The Christian's Vital Breath

An Anthology on Prayer

Ralph I. Tilley, Editor

LITS Books
P. O. Box 405
Sellersburg, Indiana 47172

Ralph I. Tilley is the executive director of Life in the Spirit Ministries and online
editor of Life in the Spirit Journal. For further information, contact . . .

litsjournal.org
editor@litsjournal.org

This volume is affectionately dedicated to
Sharon, Gordon, Dorothy and Mary —
my four praying siblings.

With gratitude to those who proofread
various portions of this volume:
Emily — my wife,
Philip Estes — a septuagenarian friend,
Frances Kinlaw Moore — a nonagenarian friend.

Contents

Introduction

It has now been over a half-century since my conversion to Christ. I rose from the church altar that Sunday evening (an altar that had not only been stained a mahogany color when it was first constructed, but had been stained through the years with the penitential tears of sinners and weeping saints alike) knowing that my sins had been forgiven, and that I should go to Bible college to begin preparation for vocational ministry. I had been sovereignly chosen to preach the unsearchable riches of Christ.

Since I arrived at the school campus unannounced and after midnight, with the men's dorm yet unopened, I spent my first night sleeping on the floor of a vacant school apartment. A friend had accompanied me to this Christian institution, though himself making no profession of faith at the time. After we lay down on our makeshift beds, David quietly announced, "You know, Ralph, if you're going to be a preacher, you need to pray before we go to sleep." So I prayed.

My mother was a praying person, so prayers were a regular ritual in our home. Prayers were offered before meals—always by mom; prayers were offered before we were sent off to school; and mom was often heard praying in her "closet." The saints prayed at church—always on their knees; and the pastor always knelt in prayer when he first ascended the platform, from which he preached.

Writers, like lawyers, will on occasion make what appears to be an exaggerated statement in order to drive home a point. Eugene Peterson—author of many devotional-theological books, as well as being the para-translator of *The Message*—once made such an extreme remark: "We don't need more Bible studies," so said the pastor-preacher-theologian.

Having read after Peterson for many years, I'm quite certain he isn't opposed to studying the Bible—he himself studied and taught the Bible for many years. But, as I recall, the point he was driving home was that Christians and churches have lost their devotional balance—the balance between study and prayer.

If one is disinclined to agree with such an assertion, just take a serious look at your own prayer life and that of your church's. How much time are we giving to the study of the Scriptures in comparison to concentrated, meaningful prayer times? How often do we set aside time to be alone with God in undistracted communion? I'm not talking about *hours* in prayer, though that may occasionally occur. We need to ask ourselves: What place does prayer have in my own life and my family's? For the church, what we call "Prayer Breakfasts" are often ninety-eight per cent breakfast and two percent prayer. What we call midweek prayer meetings are regularly seventy-five percent Bible studies and singing and fifteen percent prayer—if that, and then much of the praying focuses on material/physical concerns. And what has become of meaningful, substantive pastoral prayers in our worship services?

While we are teaching many necessary things in our Sunday schools, Bible colleges and seminaries, who is teaching God's people how to pray? When meeting with the architects, elders and deacons about the building of new facilities, who speaks up and says, "We must have at least one room designated as a prayer room"? We have kitchens, dining rooms, and gymnasiums. Where is the prayer room? And if we had one, would it be used?

God has always had a remnant throughout the centuries who, in taking God's written words seriously, took talking with God, communing with God, struggling with God, and pleading with God just as seriously—by means of this thing called prayer. One cannot read about Enoch, Noah, Abraham, Hannah, David and Daniel, Anna and Mary, Stephen and Paul, John and James, Epaphras and Timothy—and a host of praying saints throughout the church's history—without being impressed with the importance that prayer and solitude played in their walk with God.

God's authentic people have always been praying people, following the supreme example of the Lord Jesus. Great works of God have been built through the intercessions of God's servants. God's work always moves most effectively when the people of God are on their knees as much as they are in business meetings. The church's wise men have always known this: "The effective prayer of a righteous man can accomplish much" (James 5:16 NASB).

Bishop Cassels (1858-1925) was the first Anglican bishop to China; he was schooled in the worth of prayer. He knew well that if peoples steeped in centuries of myth and superstition were to be taken captive for the Kingdom, the walls of resistance could only be broken down by believing prayer. "We must advance upon our knees," said Cassels, in view of the needs and the possibilities of that vast country. "There must be a fresh taking hold of God in prayer. . . . I thank God that this mission lives upon prayer. But I say, God will do a *new thing* for us when there is a new spirit of prayer among us. God will do a *new thing* for us when there is a new spirit of consecration among us."[1] Yes, "God will do a *new thing* for us when there is a new spirit of prayer among us" — the *Spirit* of prayer! When God breathes his Spirit within us, we will respond in prayer as naturally as breathing itself.

One of the masters on this subject of prayer was South African, Andrew Murray (1828-1917). "Prayer has often been compared to breathing," wrote Murray in his classic volume on the subject, "we have only to carry out the comparison fully to see how wonderful the place is which the Holy Spirit occupies. With every breath we expel the impure air which would soon cause our death, and inhale again the fresh air to which we owe our life. So we give out from us, in confession the sins, in prayer the needs and the desires of our heart. And in drawing in our breath again, we inhale the fresh air of the promises, and the love, and the life of God in Christ." Then Murray insightfully remarks, "We do this through the Holy Spirit, who is the breath of our life." Then, adding, "just as on every expiration there follows again the inhaling or drawing in of the breath, so God draws in again His breath, and the Spirit returns to Him laden with the desires and needs of our hearts."[2]

A praying person is an awful weapon in the hands of God. Prayer — believing, Spirit-directed, truth-based prayer — glorifies God, exalts the Lord Jesus Christ, honors the blessed Holy Spirit, and builds the church up the way Christ intends it to be built.

True praying is as necessary to the growth of the Christian and the growth of the church as breathing is to the life and health of the human body. Because this is so, Scottish Moravian hymn writer, James Montgomery (1771-1854), wrote,

> *Prayer is the Christian's vital breath,*
> *the Christian's native air . . .*[3]

Most of the following chapters originally appeared in *Life in the Spirit Journal*. They are written by a variety of authors, including this editor. How I thank God that the Lord Jesus has shown us the way of prayer, as well as many noble saints who have walked in his footsteps. In the words of Frances Ridley Havergal (1836-1879):

> *There are noble Christian workers,*
> *The men of faith and power,*
> *The overcoming wrestlers*
> *Of many a midnight hour;*
> *Prevailing princes with their God,*
> *Who will not be denied,*
> *Who bring down showers of blessing*
> *To swell the rising tide.*
> *The Prince of Darkness quaileth*
> *At their triumphant way,*
> *Their fervent prayer availeth*
> *To sap his subtle way.*

If anyone is inclined to think that some of the contents in this volume sound rather extreme on this subject of prayer, possibly we need to examine our own prayer life, allowing our merciful Lord to stir us up to take this matter more seriously. After all, prayer is "the Christian's vital breath."

Be encouraged; the Spirit indwells you and will increasingly teach you how to pray!

Ralph I. Tilley, Editor
Soli Deo Gloria

1

This Thing Called Prayer

Ralph I. Tilley

Between Adam's recorded conversation with his Creator-God in the Garden of Eden, to the Apostle John's dialogue with Christ on Patmos (Genesis to Revelation), the sacred Scriptures contain a plethora of references to this subject of prayer. The Old Testament records many narratives of patriarchs, prophets, priests, and kings in prayer to God, as well as occasions when the common man and woman is found praying. The Psalter is a book of recorded prayers. In the New Testament, the Gospels—especially Luke—emphasize the importance of prayer in the life and ministry of the Lord Jesus Christ. The book of Acts has many references to individual believers calling upon God, as well as noting many accounts when believers gathered for corporate prayer. In the Epistles, there are several of Paul's prayers preserved, as well as repeated exhortations to believers—urging them to pray for a variety of reasons. The book of Revelation contains references to John praying to Christ, and angels worshiping God the Father and the enthroned Lamb. One cannot read the Scriptures without noticing the importance that its Author gives to this subject.

While the topic of prayer is vast, and many facets of the subject of prayer could be explored, I will address only a few in this chapter: What Is Prayer?, Why Does God Want Us to Pray?, Does Prayer Change Things?, Praying in Jesus' Name, and Praying in Faith.

It was the Apostle James who knew from both observation and experience, "The effective prayer of a righteous man can accomplish

1

much" (James 5:16 NASB). Every Christian should aspire to be an effective pray-er. "Lord, teach us to pray."

What is Prayer?

According to James M. Boice (1938-2000), "By prayer we speak to God."[1] In the words of Dallas Willard (1935-2013), "Prayer is conversing, communicating with God. When we pray we talk to God, aloud or within our thoughts."[2] Bingham Hunter says prayer is "communication from whole persons to the Wholeness which is the living God."[3] James Hastings (1852-1922), in his classic volume on prayer, says prayer includes desire, communion, and petition.[4]

Does the Bible itself provide us with a definition of prayer? Not really. The Bible does record a variety of prayers, prayed under a variety of circumstances,,by a wide range of praying people; it contains many exhortations and invitations by God to pray, but the Bible doesn't give us a definition *per se*. The Bible describes what prayer is and tells us how we should pray, but nowhere does it offer us a comprehensive *statement* that embraces the totality of prayer's essence. However, although the Scriptures do not give us a so-called *definition* of prayer, they do provide us with particular terms and concepts from which we can construct the meaning and essence of prayer, as well as offering significant examples of praying men and women.

One of the most helpful books I've reviewed on this study is a section in James Garrett's *Systematic Theology,* that addresses the subject of prayer at some length. Garrett explores the meaning of OT and NT terms used for prayer. He says the OT contains more than seventy occurrences of the verb *pãllal and* over seventy of the cognate noun *tᵉpîlãh*. According to Garrett's study, the verb "in the piel stem means to 'think,' 'suppose,' or 'judge,' whereas in the hithpael stem it means 'to supplicate, 'pray,' or 'intercede for.'"[5] An example of the verbal form is located in Numbers 11:2: "Then the people cried out to Moses, and Moses prayed to the LORD, and the fire died down."[6] An example of the noun form is found in a prayer of King Solomon, 1 Kings 8:28, "Yet have regard to the prayer of your servant and to his plea, O LORD my God" (1 Kings 8:28). From the NT, Garrett cites nine terms that express the experience of prayer, found in the table bellow.[7]

Greek Term	Meaning	Bible Reference Examples
euchomai (verb)	to pray (to God), to wish for	"they...*prayed* for day to come" (Acts 27:29).
proseuchomai (verb)	to pray	"When you *pray*" (Luke 11:2).
proseuchē (noun)	prayer offered to God	"My house will be called a house of *prayer*" (Mark 11:17).
denomai (verb)	to lack, to desire, to ask or beg, to pray	"... *pray earnestly to* the Lord of the harvest" (Matt. 9:38).
deēsis (noun)	entreating, prayer, supplication	"The *prayer* of a righteous person has great power" (James 5:16).
erotaō (verb)	to ask, beseech, to pray	"And I will *ask* the Father, and he will give you another Helper" (John 14:16).
entygchanō (verb)	to intercede	"... the Spirit *intercedes* for the saints according to the will of God" (Rom. 8:27).
hyperentygchanō (verb)	to intercede	"... the Spirit *helps* us in our weaknesses" (Rom 8:26).
parakaleō (verb)	to call to one's side, to speak to, to admonish, to entreat, to console	"Do you think I cannot *appeal* to my Father ...?" (Matt. 26).

From the above examples and citations, it is clear that prayer covers a wide range of expressions in communication with God. As is often the case, what is difficult to express in prose, might better be stated in poetry. Scottish Moravian hymn writer, James Montgomery (1771-1854), comes as close as any extrabiblical writer I've read, when he penned the following words about this thing called prayer:

Prayer is the soul's sincere desire,
*   unuttered or expressed;*
The motion of a hidden fire
*   that trembles in the breast.*
Prayer is the burden of a sigh,
*   the falling of a tear,*

3

The upward glancing of an eye,
*   when none but God is near.*

Prayer is the simplest form of speech
*   that infant lips can try;*
Prayer, the sublimest strains that reach
*   The Majesty on high.*

Prayer is the contrite sinner's voice,
*   returning from his ways,*
While angels in their songs rejoice
*   and cry, "Behold, he prays!"*

The saints in prayer appear as one
*   in word, in deed, and mind,*
While with the Father and the Son
*   sweet fellowship they find.*

No prayer is made by man alone
*   the Holy Spirit pleads,*
And Jesus, on th' eternal throne,
*   for sinners intercedes.*

Prayer is the Christian's vital breath,
*   the Christian's native air,*
His watchword at the gates of death;
*   he enters heaven with prayer.*

O thou, by whom we come to God,
*   the Life, the Truth, the Way;*
The path of prayer thyself hast trod:
*   Lord, teach us how to pray!* [8]

Yes, Christian prayer is the spirit of man reaching out to the God and Father of the Lord Jesus Christ, through the Holy Spirit, whether in a sigh or groan, a fleeting thought or extended intercourse. It can be expressed by praise or petition, gratitude or adoration, intercession or meditation. Prayer is communion; prayer is worship. Whether it is of-fered in public or in private, silently or vocally, if the heart is directed toward God — that is prayer.

Why Does God Want Us to Pray?

Why is it that God wants the highest of all his creation to pray? This question sounds rather impertinent when we think about it. It is like asking a father why he wants his child to talk with him. Because prayer in its simplest form is redeemed men and women talking to, communing with God, it stands to reason why our God and Father would desire that his children communicate with Him.

This is not to suggest that God, as the self-existent, self-sufficient eternal Being, has any *need* in himself for man to pray to him — God does not experience *need*. However, when he made man, he made man in his image, and one of the features of this divine image is communion, spirit interacting with spirit. This is also true of the Three-in-One God. From all eternity, the Father, Son, and Holy Spirit have engaged and delighted in holy conversation. For example, communion among the persons of the Trinity is implicit in the words, "Let *us* make man in our image, after our likeness" (Gen. 1:26). The use of the first person plural indicates a plural of persons in Deity. We know that as God revealed more and more of himself to the prophets and apostles, that this One God is a tri-unity, a trinity.

Made in the image of God, men and women have been created to have fellowship with their Creator-Redeemer, and the primary instrument of that fellowship is prayer — man talking to God in response to God's revelation of himself.

Since behind all sincere prayer is a sense of man's own helplessness, inability and dependence, God desires that man should respond to this innate need for him and pray. "God wants us to pray," notes Wayne Grudem, "because prayer expresses our trust in God and is a means whereby our trust in him can increase. In fact, perhaps the primary emphasis of the Bible's teaching on prayer is that we are to pray with faith, which means trust or dependence on God."[9] God also wants us to pray, observes Grudem, because "prayer brings us into a deeper fellowship with God" as well as allowing "us as creatures to be involved in activities that are eternally important."[10] Prayer is an expression of our dependence on God, a means of fellowship, and means of furthering Kingdom purposes. God extends this medium of communication to all who will hear: "You have said, 'Seek my face.' My heart says to you, 'Your face, LORD, do I seek'" (Psa. 27:8).

Does Prayer Change Things?

It has often been a subject of discussion among Bible scholars on the subject of prayer as to whether or not prayer actually *changes* things. Quaker Richard Foster posits that believing prayer has the capacity of changing both people and things. On the matter of changing people, Foster says, "Real prayer is life creating and life changing. . . . To pray is to change. Prayer is the central avenue God uses to transform us. If we are unwilling to change, we will abandon prayer as a noticeable characteristic of our lives."[11] When it comes to prayer's power to change things, Foster says, "Certain things will happen in history if we pray rightly. We are to change the world by prayer."[12]

Writing from a Reformed perspective, Millard Erickson considers the matter of providence and prayer a "problem": "One problem that has concerned thoughtful Christians when considering the nature of providence is the role of prayer. This dilemma stems from the question of what prayer really accomplishes."[13] Erickson goes on to reason that if prayer has any outcome on what happens, then "God's plan was not fixed in the first place." If, on the other hand, "God's will is established and he will do what he is going to do, then does it matter whether we pray?" Erickson views this subject as a "larger issue of the relationship between human effort and divine providence." He believes two biblical truths must be kept in mind whenever one prays: " 1) Scripture teaches that God's plan is definite and fixed — it is not subject to revision; and 2) we are commanded to pray and taught that prayer has value."

How does Erickson resolve this tension? His reading of Scripture causes him to conclude "that in many cases God works in a sort of partnership with humans. God does not act if humans do not play their part." After citing a few miracles Jesus performed in response to the faith of individuals — for example, the healing of the centurion's servant and the lady with a hemorrhage — Erickson concludes: "When God wills the end (in these cases), he also wills the means (which includes a request to be healed, which in turn presupposes faith). Thus prayer does not change what he purposed to do. It is the means by which he accomplishes his end." What role does prayer play in these matters then? Erickson says, "It is vital, then, that a prayer be uttered, for without it the desired result will not come to pass."

Writing from a Lutheran perspective, Ole Hallesby (1879-1961) wrote a volume on prayer that is now regarded as a classic. As to whether or not prayer changes *things*, Hallesby states, "From the Scriptures and from our own experience we are certain that prayer changes things with respect to the way God governs, not only individuals, but society, the nations and the whole world."[14] As to how this can be so, Hallesby reasons: "When God changes the divine world-economy as a result of man's prayers, we mean that He governs the world with such a degree of elasticity that He can alter His methods as circumstances here below require, be they good or bad. He does not alter His kingdom-plans, only the means and methods whereby He at each moment seeks to accomplish them. God takes immediate cognizance, therefore, of man's prayer in His government of the world. Something does take place as a result of man's prayer, which otherwise would not take place."[15] I would offer a clear "Amen" to Hallesby's assertion: "Something does take place as a result of man's prayer, which otherwise would not take place."

It is plain from Scripture that God wants us to petition him and to even persevere in offering our petitions. To Jeremiah, God said, "Call to me and I will answer you and will tell you great and hidden things that you have not known" (Jer. 33:3). In his Sermon on the Mount, the Lord Jesus encouraged his disciples to persevere in making their petitions: "Ask, and it will be given to you; seek, and you will find; knock, and it will be opened to you. For everyone who asks receives, and the one who seeks finds, and to the one who knocks it will be opened" (Matt. 7:7-8). The verbs—"ask," seek" and "knock" are in the imperfect tense, suggesting one should "keep asking," "keep seeking," "keep knocking."

Of course, what must be assumed in our prayer-petitions is the *will of God* in the matter, and the *right motives* in our praying. On the will of God, the Apostle John wrote, "And this is the confidence that we have toward him, that if we ask anything according to his will he hears us. And if we know that he hears us in whatever we ask, we know that we have the requests that we have asked of him" (1 John 5:14-15). On the importance of having the right motives in offering our petitions, the Apostle James says, "You ask and do not receive, because you ask wrongly" (James 4:3). The classic text, of course, when it comes to this matter of praying in harmony with the will of God is the prayer of our

Lord in Gethsemane's Garden: "Father, if you are willing, remove this cup from me. Nevertheless, not my will, but yours, be done" (Luke 22:42).

The Scriptures clearly teach—at least it is clear to me—that God uses the prayers of his believing people, who pray according to his will, to effect change. How else can one explain, for example, God's answering the earnest cry of King Hezekiah when he became deathly ill. Isaiah delivered God's word to the king: "Thus says the LORD, 'Set your house in order, for you shall die; you shall not recover'" (Is 20:1). But Hezekiah did not die and did recover. Why? Because God looked with favor upon the king's humble petition for healing. Following the king's fervent request for healing, God directed Isaiah to return to the king and inform him that his prayer had been answered: "Thus says the LORD, the God of David your father: I have heard your prayer; I have seen your tears. Behold, I will heal you" (Isa. 20:5). On the one hand, God said the king would die; on the other hand—in answer to the king's prayer—God said the king would live. Did God have a will in both Hezekiah's illness and his healing. Surely he did. Was God's will done? We must conclude it was. Within his will, does God invite his children to occasionally intercede with him so as to *change* his *revealed* will? It appears so. Is there such a thing as God's declaring a conclusion, an outcome about a matter so as to never accept the prayers of even the godliest of people? Yes. God told Ezekiel on one occasion: "Son of man, when a land sins against me by acting faithlessly, and I stretch out my hand against it and break its supply of bread and send famine upon it, and cut off from it man and beast, even if these three men, Noah, Daniel, and Job, were in it, they would deliver but their own lives by their righteousness, declares the Lord GOD" (Ezek. 14:13-14). Karl Barth (1886-1968) likened God's altering His "intentions" (and changing his mind) with that of his stooping to man's weakness in the incarnation of Christ, thereby demonstrating his greatness:

> The fact that God yields to human petitions, that he alters his intentions and follows the bent of our prayers, is not a sign of weakness. In his own majesty and in the splendor of his might, he has willed and yet wills it so. He desires to be the God who has been made flesh in Jesus Christ. Therein lies his glory, his omnipotence. He does not then impair himself by yielding to

our prayer; on the contrary, it is in so doing that he shows his greatness.

If God himself wishes to enter into fellowship with human-kind and be close to us as a father is to his child, he does not thereby weaken his might. God cannot be greater than he is in Jesus Christ. If God answers our prayer, it is not then only because he listens to us and increases our faith (the efficacy of prayer has sometimes been explained in this manner), but because he is God: Father, Son, and Holy Spirit, God whose word has been made flesh.[16]

Praying in Jesus' Name

Jesus told the disciples in his farewell instructions, that following his departure and the Spirit's descent, they were to offer their petitions "in His name":

"Whatever you ask *in my name*, this I will do, that the Father may be glorified in the Son. If you ask me anything *in my name*, I will do it" (John 14:13-14, emphasis added).

"You did not choose me, but I chose you and appointed you that you should go and bear fruit and that your fruit should abide, so that whatever you ask the Father *in my name*, he may give it to you" (John 15:16, emphasis added).

"In that day you will ask nothing of me. Truly, truly, I say to you, whatever you ask of the Father *in my name*, he will give it to you. [24] Until now you have asked nothing *in my name*. Ask, and you will receive, that your joy may be full" (John 16:23-24, emphasis added).

"In that day you will ask *in my name*, and I do not say to you that I will ask the Father on your behalf" (John 16:26, emphasis added).

While the phrase, "in Jesus' name," is routinely added at the end of Christian prayers (sometimes one is led to believe, mindlessly so), what is its actual significance? What does it mean to pray *in Jesus' name*?

Though Jesus never explained to his disciples what he meant by praying in his name, the English Methodist Evangelical, Samuel Chadwick (1860-1932), said the "meaning was plain enough to every Israelite. God was in His Name. . . . The name expresses personality, character, and Being. The Person is the Name. Prayer in Christ's name is prayer according to the quality of His Person, according to the character of His mind, and according to His will and purpose."[17] To pray "in Jesus' name," according to Carl Henry (1913-2003), means to pray "in accord with the revelation of God's character and purpose manifest in the Nazarene."[18] To pray "in Jesus' name," according to W. T. Purkiser (1910-1992), means at least four things. It "means approaching God in full awareness of the mediatorship of the Son and of the free access opened by the Son. It implies an abandonment of any conceit that we are worthy to approach a holy God on our own merits. It also means coming in harmony with the character of the Son — always implied by name, in biblical usage." Furthermore, Purkiser says it also means "coming in dependence upon the authority of the Son."[19] In stressing this truth in John 14-16 to his disciples, Herman Ridderbos (1909-2007) says, "Jesus is pledging that he is not withdrawing from them by his departure but will be able, because of his heavenly glory, to give them everything they will need for the continuation of his work on earth, and he refers them to prayer as the way of his continuing fellowship with them."[20]

In the OT we have many references to people calling upon "the name of the Lord." For example, Abram "built an altar to the LORD and called upon the name of the LORD" (Gen. 12:8). Later, following his change of name, we read where Abraham "planted a tamarisk tree in Beersheba and called there on the name of the LORD, the Everlasting God" (Gen. 21:33).

Furthermore, with the Hebrew people, one's name reflected one's character and sometimes one's calling. Following his all-night struggle with the angel at Jabbok's brook, God changed Jacob's name from "Jacob" (meaning "deceiver") to "Israel" (meaning "he struggles with God"). After seeing the "face of God" at Peniel (which is what "Peniel" means), Jacob was a changed man, thus receiving a new name from God (see Gen. 32:22-32).

God's name reflects his nature, character, attributes, and his activity in redemption. For example, when God revealed himself to Moses, he said, "I am the LORD [*Yahweh*]. I appeared to Abraham, to Isaac, and to Jacob, as God Almighty [*El-Shaddai*], but by my name the LORD [*Yahweh*] I did not make myself known to them" (Ex. 6:2-3). Later, when God revealed himself to Moses, we read, "The LORD [*Yahweh*] descended in the cloud and stood with him there, and proclaimed the name of the LORD [*Yahweh*]. The LORD [*Yahweh*] passed before him and proclaimed, "The LORD [*Yahweh*], the LORD [*Yahweh*], a God merciful and gracious, slow to anger, and abounding in steadfast love and faithfulness, keeping steadfast love for thousands, forgiving iniquity and transgression and sin, but who will by no means clear the guilty, visiting the iniquity of the fathers on the children and the children's children, to the third and the fourth generation" (Ex. 34:5-7). Here God's name—"LORD" [*Yahweh*]—represents God's compassion and grace, patience with sinners, and abounding love, faithfulness, and justice.

Therefore, when Jesus informed his disciples that following his departure they were to offer their prayers in his name, he was saying that as their future Mediator, they could pray with the confident expectation that their prayers would be heard and answered because his holy character would deliver whatever he had promised — in harmony with his will.

Praying in Faith

If our prayers are to be answered by God, the Scriptures teach that one of the essential components on the part of the petitioner is that of faith—faith that God will answer the requested petition, according to his promised Word. The Hebrews' writer underscores this fundamental fact when he says, "And without faith it is impossible to please him, for whoever would draw near to God must believe that he exists and that he rewards those who seek him" (Heb. 11:6). Jesus repeatedly taught the necessity of prayers being offered to God in the belief that our Father in Heaven would favorably grant the desired petition. Of the two blind men who approached Jesus requesting that he give them their sight, Jesus asked, "Do you believe I am able to do this?" (Matt. 9:28). Following the cursing of the fig tree and the subsequent surprise by his disciples upon seeing the withered plant, Jesus said, "whatever you ask in prayer, you will receive, if you have faith" (Matt. 21:22). On another occasion, Jesus assured his disciples, "whatever you ask in prayer, believe that you have received it, and it will be yours" (Mark 11:24).

Following many of the healing miracles Jesus performed, he told the healed people that it was because of their faith that he was able to answer their requests. For example, after Jesus healed the centurion's servant, Jesus announced, "Truly, I tell you, with no one in Israel have I found such faith" Matt. 8:10). After healing the woman with a hemorrhage, Jesus said to her, "Daughter, your faith has made you well; go in peace, and be healed of your disease" (Mark 5:34). The people went away saying it was *Jesus* who healed them; Jesus said it was because of their *faith* they were healed.

Faith, according to Hebrews 11:1, is "the assurance of things hoped for, the conviction of things not seen." Such "biblical faith," according to Grudem, "is never a kind of wishful thinking or a vague hope that does not have any secure foundation to rest upon. It is rather trust in a person, God himself, based on the fact that we take him at his word and believe what he has said. This trust or dependence on God, when it has an element of assurance or confidence, is genuine biblical faith."[21]

Conclusion

Having limited my scope on the subject of prayer in this chapter to five areas—What Is Prayer? Why Does God Want Us to Pray? Does Prayer Change Things? Praying in Jesus' Name, and Praying in Faith — I have not explored many other facets. Nonetheless, it should reaffirm to the reader the importance of walking in close communion with our Lord, and understanding that our God eagerly awaits to answer the prayers of his believing children. It was the Apostle James who stated, "The effective prayer of a righteous man can accomplish much" (James 5:16 NASB). The Lord continually reminds me through his Word and the writings of others, that I should not hesitate to ask largely of him, that he wants me to make my requests known to him in believing prayer. By his grace I shall. In closing, I want to share one of my favorite hymns on this subject of prayer. Written by John Newton (1725-1807), it challenges me each time I read it.

Come, my soul, thy suit prepare:
Jesus loves to answer prayer;
He Himself has bid thee pray,

Therefore will not say thee nay.

Thou art coming to a King,
Large petitions with thee bring;
For His grace and power are such,
None can ever ask too much.

With my burden I begin:
Lord, remove this load of sin;
Let Thy blood, for sinners spilt,
Set my conscience free from guilt.

Lord, I come to Thee for rest,
Take possession of my breast;
There Thy blood bought right maintain,
And without a rival reign.

As the image in the glass
Answers the beholder's face;
Thus unto my heart appear,
Print Thine own resemblance there.

While I am a pilgrim here,
Let Thy love my spirit cheer;
As my Guide, my Guard, my Friend,
Lead me to my journey's end.

Show me what I have to do,
Every hour my strength renew:
Let me live a life of faith,
Let me die Thy people's death.[22]

2

A Prayer to Christ

Anselm of Canterbury

O good Christ, O Lord Jesus, . . . neither seeking Thee, nor thinking of Thee, Thou didst shine upon me like a sun, and didst show me in what predicament I was.

Thou didst throw away the leaden weight that dragged me down; Thou didst take off the burden that weighed upon me; Thou didst drive back the pursuing foes, and stand forth against them in my defense; Thou calledst me by a new name, a name which Thou gavest me after Thine own; and, bowed down as I was, didst raise and set me up so as to behold Thee, saying, "Be of good heart; I have redeemed thee, I have given My life for thee. Do but cleave to Me, and thou shalt escape the miseries in which thou wast, and shalt not fall into the deep whither thou wast hurrying; but I will lead thee on, even to My kingdom, and make thee an heir of God, and a joint-heir with Myself."

Thenceforth Thou didst take me into Thy keeping, that nothing should hurt my soul against Thy allowing. And, behold, although as yet I have not clung to Thee as Thou didst counsel, yet Thou hast not let me fall into hell, but art waiting still, that I may cling to Thee, and Thou do for me as Thou hast promised. In truth, O

Lord, such was my condition, and thus hast Thou dealt with me. I was in darkness; for I knew nothing, not even myself. I was on slippery ground; for I was weak and frail, and prone to slip into sin.

I was on the slopes over the pit of hell; for I had lapsed in my first parents from justice to injustice, a road by which men travel down into hell; and from beatitude to temporal woe, whence men launch into eternal.

The weight of original sin drew me from below, and the unsupportable burden of God's judgment oppressed me from above; and my foes the demons, that by fresh actual sins they might make me more worthy of damnation, vehemently assailed me as much as in them it lay to do. Thus destitute, thus helpless, Thou, Jesus, didst shine upon me, and show me in what state I was. For even when as yet I could not know or be aware of it, Thou didst teach it all to others, who were to learn in my behalf, and afterwards me myself, or ever I sought it of Thee.

The dragging lead, the pressing load, the urging foes Thou hast rid me of them all; for Thou hast taken away the sin in which I was conceived and born, both the sin and its condemnation, and hast warded off the spiteful fiends from doing violence to my soul.

Thou hast caused me to be called after Thy Name, a Christian; the Name by which I make confession of Thee, and Thou too dost own me among Thy redeemed; Thou hast lifted me up, moreover, and raised me to the knowledge and the love of Thee; Thou hast made me have good hope for the salvation of my soul, my soul for which Thou gavest Thine, and, only that I follow Thee, hast promised me Thy glory. And lo, although not yet I follow Thee as Thou hast counselled nay, rather, have committed many sins which Thou hast forbidden still Thou dost wait, dost wait that I may follow Thee, dost wait to give what Thou hast promised.[1]

3

The Meaning of Prayer

Ole Hallesby

About twenty years ago I made a fairly extended trip into Germany for the purpose of studying there. After having worked hard for some time, I had decided to take a little vacation. Accordingly, I planned a trip to Switzerland to pay a visit to the old patriarch, Samuel Zeller (1834-1912), in Mannedorf. He conducted a "spiritual sanatorium" on the shores of Lake Zürich for people who desired rest, not only for their bodies, but also for their souls.

Zeller was an unusually gifted man, both by nature as well as by spiritual endowment. He was an excellent organizer and had succeeded in gradually building up a large institute for the care of people who were mentally or physically ill, tired, or worn out nervously.

He was an outstanding speaker. I have heard men with greater natural ability as speakers, but I have never heard any one who has surpassed Zeller as a preacher. He succeeded in accomplishing what should be the real objective in all preaching: to bring the listeners into the presence of God by means of the Word. It was as though all else faded away and we stood in the presence of God alone when Zeller spoke.

He was exceptional also as a pastor. I, at least, have never met anyone in whom such a profound knowledge of human nature was coupled with such tender, sympathetic love.

Lastly, he had received the extraordinary gift of grace of healing by prayer. By the prayer of faith he was able to help a large number of

17

people and set them free from many a physical and spiritual infirmity.

And yet none of these things made the deepest impression upon me. My strongest impression was that of Zeller in prayer.

I do not think that I exaggerate when I say that I have never heard anyone pray as he did, although I have heard many who were more emotional and more fervent when they prayed. Zeller, on the contrary, was quiet and confident while he prayed. He knew God well, and for that reason he was confident.

I do not believe that I have ever heard any one expect so much of God and so little of his own prayers as he did. He merely told God what was needed. He knew that God would take care of the rest. His prayers were reverent, but natural, conversations with God, as though God were sitting in the first pew and Zeller were standing before Him.

Zeller had much to pray for when we assembled for morning devotionals. First, he prayed for our fellowship, then for the whole institution with all its aged and infirm patients, and finally for all the sick and unfortunate everywhere who had sent him letters asking for intercession. During the short time that I was there letters came to him from every country in Europe, with the exception of Norway and Sweden.

Thus he prayed every day for many people and for many things. But as I listened to these prayers of his I had to say to myself, "After all he prays only one prayer, namely, that the name of God might be glorified."

Oftentimes he prayed for miracles. But never without adding, "If it will glorify Thy name." Nor was he afraid to pray for instantaneous healing, but always with the provision mentioned above.

He made no attempt to dictate to God or to force Him by His own promises. Miracle-working prayer was not to Zeller a means of escaping tribulation; it was only a means of glorifying the name of God.

For that reason he would often say, "If it will glorify Thy name more, then let them remain sick; but, if that be Thy will, give them power to glorify Thy name through their illness."

And he did not only pray that way for others. He who had been instrumental in healing others, was himself afflicted with a dangerous internal ailment, which might at any time cause his own painful death. He knew that he was called to glorify God through his ailment.

Here the purpose and meaning of prayer dawned upon me for the first time. Here I was privileged to see more clearly than ever before the purpose of prayer: to glorify the name of God.

The scales fell from my eyes. I saw in a new light the misuse of prayer and the difficulties connected with prayer as well as the place of our own efforts in prayer.

Prayer life has its own laws, as all the rest of life has. The fundamental law in prayer is this: prayer is given and ordained for the purpose of glorifying God. Prayer is the appointed way of giving Jesus an opportunity to exercise His supernatural powers of salvation. And in so doing He desires to make use of us.

We should through prayer give Jesus the opportunity of gaining access to our souls, our bodies, our homes, our neighborhoods, our countries, to the whole world, to the fellowship of believers and to the unsaved.

If we will make use of prayer, not to wrest from God advantages for ourselves or our dear ones, or to escape from tribulations and difficulties, but to call down upon ourselves and others those things which will glorify the name of God, then we shall see the strongest and boldest promises of the Bible about prayer fulfilled also in our weak, little prayer life. Then we shall see such answers to prayer as we had never thought were possible.

It is written, "And this is the boldness which we have toward him, that, if we ask anything according to his will, he heareth us: and if we know that he heareth us whatsoever we ask, we know that we have the petitions which we ask of him" (1 John 5:14-15).

The apostle establishes the fact from his own prayer experience as well as that of his readers, that if we pray for anything according to the will of God, we already have what we pray for the moment we ask it. It is immediately sent from Heaven on its way to us. We do not know exactly when it will arrive while we are asking for it; but he who has learned to know God through the Spirit of God, has learned to leave this in His hands, and to live just as happily whether the answer arrives immediately or later.

By this time no doubt some of my sincere praying readers are feeling depressed. After what has been said so far, you are beginning to suspect that you have misunderstood and misused the sacred privilege of prayer altogether. You have in your daily prayer life been speaking with God about everything, about greater as well as lesser things. You have even asked Him for most insignificant things. And you are afraid that this is a misuse of prayer, and that you should therefore cease at once. A deep sigh arises from your heart.

Nay, my friend, you should by no means cease. On the contrary, you should pray God for still greater simplicity of mind in your daily conversation with Him. Pray that you may become so confidential with Him that you can speak with Him about everything in your daily life. That is what He desires. That is just how He would have us pray. You will no doubt recall that it is written, "In nothing be anxious; but in everything by prayer and supplication with thanksgiving let your requests be made known unto God" (Phil. 4:6).

He knows that it is in our daily lives that we most easily become anxious. He knows, too, that our daily lives are made up of little things, not great things. Therefore He beckons to us in a friendly way and says, "Just bring all those little things to me; I am most willing to help you."

Be sure to remember that nothing in your daily life is so insignificant and so inconsequential that the Lord will not help you by answering your prayer. Some day you may perhaps be looking for some keys that you have lost. You must have them, and you are in a hurry, and you cannot find them. Go trustingly to God and tell Him about your predicament. Or, perhaps your little boy is out playing. You need him at once to run an errand for you. But you cannot take the time to look for him or to run the errand yourself. Tell it confidently to your Father in Heaven.

Do not forget, however, what we mentioned above, that prayer is ordained for the purpose of glorifying the name of God. Therefore, whether you pray for big things or for little things, say to God, "If it will glorify Thy name, then grant my prayer and help me. But if it will not glorify Thy name, then let me remain in my predicament. And give me power to glorify Thy name in the situation in which I find myself."

Some may think that this will weaken the power and the intensity of our prayers. But this is due to a misunderstanding of prayer as a whole. To pray is to let Jesus come into our need. And only by praying in this way will we succeed in opening our hearts to Jesus. This will give Him the opportunity to exercise His power on our behalf, not only as He wills but also when He wills. Peace and tranquility will then fill our hearts.

As mentioned above, restlessness in prayer comes from striving against the Spirit of prayer. But when we in prayer seek only the glorification of the name of God, then we are in complete harmony with the Spirit of prayer. Then our hearts are at rest both while we pray and after we have prayed. The reason is that we now seek by our prayers only that which will glorify the name of God.

Then we can wait for the Lord. We have learned to leave it to Him to decide what will best serve to glorify His name, either an immediate or a delayed answer to our prayer.

Permit me to cite an example to show how bold, even importunate, prayer can become when the one who is praying desires nothing but the glorification of the name of God by his supplications.

In 1540 [Martin] Luther's good friend, Friedrich Myconius (1490-1546), became deathly sick. He himself and others expected that he would die within a short time. One night he wrote with trembling hand a fond farewell to Luther, whom he loved very much.

When Luther received the letter, he sent back the following reply immediately, "I command thee in the name of God to live because I still have need of thee in the work of reforming the church. . . . The Lord will never let me hear that thou art dead, but will permit thee to survive me. For this I am praying, this is my will, and may my will be done, because I seek only to glorify the name of God."

Myconius had already lost the faculty of speech when Luther's letter came. But in a short time he was well again. And, true enough, survived Luther by two months!

Nothing makes us so bold in prayer as when we can look into the eye of God and say to Him, "Thou knowest that I am not praying for personal advantage, nor to avoid hardship, nor that my own will in any way should be done, but only for this, that Thy name might be glorified."

If we pray in this way, we shall have peace of mind also when our petitions are not granted.

At this point let us say a few words about unanswered prayers.

It cannot be denied that they cause us all a great deal of difficulty, especially our children. They have been taught to pray to Jesus, and they have been told that He is kind and good, and that He helped all who came to Him when He lived here on earth below. As a result they pray confidently to Him for everything, large and small. And they expect in all sincerity to receive that for which they have prayed.

A great crisis enters into the life of the child. The child has prayed to Jesus for something, but has not received an answer to his prayer.

Here it is necessary for us to come to the assistance of the child and explain the situation. And in speaking with children we must speak graphically; otherwise they will not be able to understand us. We must illustrate by means of examples.

We can tell them, for instance, that we have read in the papers every now and then about children who have accidentally shot themselves either with an air rifle or an ordinary gun and have become cripples for life, and that sometimes children have even been killed in that way.

How did this happen?

Because they had asked their fathers and mothers for air rifles and because they were so unfortunate as to receive what they asked for. If only their fathers and mothers had had sense enough not to give them such dangerous weapons, they would have been spared the terrible misfortune.

This will teach the child that God is merciful even when He declines to give us things that we ask of Him.

As far as that is concerned, we need to learn this lesson over and over again, because we forget so easily. We have by nature a great deal of confidence in ourselves and think that we know best what is good for us. And when God thinks differently in the matter, we suspect immediately that He is not concerned about us.

Even the Great Apostle had experiences with unanswered prayers.

Paul tells us that on one occasion he prayed three times and still did not receive what he asked for (2 Cor. 12:9-10). It was a question of an affliction which was apparently causing him a great deal of trouble in his missionary work. He prayed God to take it away from him. But God declined to heed his supplications.

This refusal was certainly not made because Paul had misused prayer by praying that the thorn in the flesh might depart from him merely in order that he might escape affliction. On the contrary, he prayed that the thorn might be removed for the sake of his missionary labors. The real purpose of his prayer was to glorify the name of God.

Nevertheless his prayer was not granted.

When Paul in this case continued to pray three times, it must have been because he was conscious that he was praying, not for personal advantage, but for the glorification of the name of God.

When God nevertheless failed to heed his supplications, it was because His name would be glorified even more by having Paul keep his affliction. By so doing, Paul would be kept humble and receptive at all times to the power of God.

Through this prayer-struggle Paul learned the great secret of fellowship with God which he expresses thus: "When I am weak, then I am strong."

Even Jesus prayed a prayer which the Father did not fulfill; and He, too, prayed three times, "Father, if it is possible, let this cup pass away from me." That was in Gethsemane, when Satan by tempting Jesus was permitted to render obscure that which all the way had been clear to Jesus, that He must suffer and die in order to save the race.

But even in the dark hour of temptation we see the pure and obedient mind of Jesus. He tells His Father candidly how He feels in temptation's darkness. But the real desire of His prayer is nevertheless this: "Not as I will, but as thou wilt."

From this we learn that we should not be afraid, when praying to God, to give expression to a definite desire, even though we are in doubt at the time we are praying whether it is really the right thing to pray for or not. Regardless of this, I say, we should pray for definite things, for those, namely, concerning which we feel a strong desire to speak to our heavenly Father. But at the same time we should do as Jesus did and add, "Nevertheless, not as I will, but as thou wilt."[1]

4

How to Pray

R. A. Torrey

There is a right way to obtain real, heart-stirring, heart-wringing, and God-moving earnestness in prayer. What the right way is the Bible tells us. It tells us in Romans 8:26-27 RV, "And in like manner the Spirit also helpeth our infirmity; for we know not how to pray as we ought; but the Spirit himself maketh intercession for us with groanings which cannot be uttered, and he that searcheth the hearts knoweth what is the mind of the Spirit, because he maketh intercession for the saints according to the will of God." That is the right way — look to the Spirit to create the earnestness. The earnestness that counts with God is not the earnestness that you or I work up; it is the earnestness that the Holy Spirit creates in our hearts.

Have you never gone to God in prayer and there was no earnestness in your prayer at all, it was just words, words, words, a mere matter of form, when it seemed there was no real prayer in your heart? What shall we do at such a time as that? Stop praying and wait until we feel more like praying? No. If there is ever a time when one needs to pray it is when he does not feel like praying. What shall we do? Be silent and look up to God to send His Holy Spirit, according to His promise, to move your heart to prayer and to awaken and create real earnestness in your heart in prayer, and God will send Him and you will pray with intense earnestness, very likely "with groanings which cannot be uttered."

I wish to testify right here that some of the times of deepest earnest-

25

ness that I have ever known in prayer came when at the outset I seemed to have no prayer in my heart at all, and all attempt to pray was mere words, words, empty form. And then I looked up to God to send His Spirit according to His promise to teach me to pray, and I waited and the Spirit of God came on me in mighty power and I cried to God, sometimes with groanings which could not be uttered.

I shall never forget a night in Chicago. After the general prayer meetings for a world-wide revival had been going on for some time, the man who was most closely associated with me in the conduct of the meetings came over to my house one night after the meeting was over and said, "Brother Torrey, what do you say to our having a time alone with God every Saturday night after the other meetings are over? I do not mean," he continued, "that we will actually promise to come to-gether every Saturday night; but let us have it tonight, anyway." Oh, such a night of prayer as we had that night. I shall never forget that, but it was not that night that I am especially thinking of now.

After we had been meeting some weeks, he suggested that we invite in a few others, which we did; and every Saturday night after the general prayer meeting was closed at ten o'clock we few would gather in some secluded place where we would not disturb others to pray to-gether. There were never more than a dozen persons present; usually there were six or seven. One night, before kneeling in prayer, we told one another the things we desired especially to ask of God that night, and then we knelt to pray and a long silence followed. No one prayed. And one of the little company looked up and said, "I cannot pray, there seems to be something resisting me." Then another raised his head and said, "Neither can I pray, something seems to be resisting me." We went around the whole circle, and each one had the same story.

What did we do? Break up the prayer meeting? No. If ever we felt the need of prayer it was then, and quietly we all bowed before God and looked to Him to send His Holy Spirit to enable us to pray to victo-ry. And soon the Spirit of God came on one and another, and I have seldom heard such praying as I heard that night. And then the Spirit of God came on me and led me out in such a prayer as I had never dreamed of praying. I was led to ask God that He would send me around die world preaching the Gospel, and give me to see thousands saved in China, in Japan, in Australia, in New Zealand, in Tasmania, in

India, in England, Scotland, Ireland, Germany, France, and Switzerland; and when I finished praying that night I knew I was going, and I knew what I would see as well as I knew afterward when the actual report came of the mighty things that God had wrought. That prayer meeting sent me around the world preaching the Gospel.

Oh, that is how we must pray if we would get what we ask in prayer—pray with the intense earnestness that the Holy Ghost alone can inspire.[1]

5

The Prayers of the Saints

Charles H. Spurgeon

"And when he had taken the scroll, the four living creatures and the twenty-four elders fell down before the Lamb, each holding a harp, and golden bowls full of incense, which are the prayers of the saints."
—Revelation 5:8

The prayers of a saint are sweet, but the prayers of *saints* are sweeter!

United prayers possess the power of harmony. In music there is melody in any one distinct note—but we have all recognized a peculiar charm in harmony.

Now, the prayers of one saint are to God melody, but the intercessions of many are harmony—and to God there is much that is pleasing in the harmony of His people's prayers.

Each Christian Prays Differently

No two children of God pray exactly alike. There is a difference of tone. If taught of God, each one will pray graciously, but there will be in one prayer what there is not in another. If all the fruits of the garden are luscious, yet each one has its own special flavor. All the bells may be of silver, and yet each one will have its own tone.

For instance, some brothers and sisters, when they pray, dwell very tenderly upon the dishonor done to God by sin. They pray as if their hearts would break and they weep at every other sentence. "O God, the idols are placed on Your Throne. Jesus is dishonored, the Law is broken, the Gospel is despised." Such loving contrition for the sin of others wails itself out in soft, low notes of magic power.

But, listen to others, and you will find their prayers pitched upon quite another key. The brother prays with full assurance that God's kingdom is established upon the mountains, where its foundation can never be removed. And though the heathens rage, and the people imagine vain things, yet surely God's kingdom and purpose will stand and He will do all His pleasure. And as you hear such petitioning, shrill and clear like the sound of a trumpet, you feel that the voice of faith is both musical and prevalent. The man has no doubt as to God's triumphing! He is quite certain that the Lord's hosts will win the day, and he prays in that spirit.

Now, if these varying tones are melted into one, what masterly harmony they make! Therefore the Lord promises great things when two of us agree as touching anything concerning His kingdom.

But, now comes in a third petitioner, and his tone of prayer differs from the other two. The same spirit of prayer is in him, but its voice varies. He prays in this way: Bowed down with a sense of awe in the presence of God, the God of all the earth, he seems to speak measuring out each word, and he cries, "O God, shall not the nations fear You? Such an One as You are, shall they not tremble in Your Presence? Will You not be King to them, O You Creator and Preserver of all things?"

Like the cherubim, he veils his face in the Presence of the excellent Glory, and your soul, by his prayer, is solemnly ushered into the Presence of God and laid prostrate there.

But mark yet this fourth man, whose prayer is of another mold: He is familiar with the Lord, he seems to have merged his sense of the sublime in that of the condescending, and he speaks somewhat in this way: "O Lord, my Father, You love the sons of men. Will You not come and meet Your prodigal sons who are coming back to You? Have You not given Jesus Christ to be a Man and bought men with Your precious blood? And will You not come to them and press them to Your bosom, and make them Yours?"

As the brother calls on God he appears to come close to Him and lay hold upon Him, and say, "I beseech You have mercy upon my fellow men."

Now, there is something blessed in both those prayers. I do not know which I prefer, but I do know, when I can get the blending of the two, the awe and the holy boldness, the familiarity and the sense of sovereignty, I find a double sweetness fills my heart!

Ah, brothers and sisters, did you ever hear a prayer of that kind which moved the Lord's heart in the wilderness — I refer to the prayer of Moses, when he said, "If not, blot my name out of the Book of Life." This is the prayer of self-sacrifice, when the man feels, "I must have God glorified. I must have these people saved. I would pawn my soul for it. I would lose myself if but this nation might be redeemed."

That is grand praying — it is not all of us who can rise to it! If that were alone and the only prayer, it might grow monotonous, for it lacks compass, but, if you put all these prayers together which I have mentioned — the prayers of the tender and the prayers of the brave, the prayers of the awe-struck and the prayers of the familiar, the prayers of the importunate, the prayers of the self-sacrificing — then they fill the golden bowl full of sweet incense!

Every Age of Life Makes a Unique Contribution in Prayer

For my part, I love, at prayer meetings, to hear the prayers of the aged. There is a lack in our prayer meetings, and has been for some months through the loss of one dear saint whose prayers used to be marrow and fatness to some of our souls on Monday evenings. The prayers of men on the verge of Heaven are to us as angels to lead us, also, up to the gates of pearl.

But it is very pleasant to hear the prayers of young people, also, even the very young, for as they talk before the Lord there is a charming simplicity and frankness too little found in others.

And then, the prayers of men in middle life, full of experiential trouble, or, on the other hand, overflowing with experienced joy! These have their peculiar aroma, and I believe God loves to see them all mixed in the golden bowls!

From Every Nation and Sector of the Body of Christ

And, what if I add He would have His people, with their various peculiarities put their prayers together? I, as a Calvinist, remark that our Arminian friends pray wonderfully Calvinistic! I can seldom perceive difference between them and ourselves, but no doubt they do view more than we do some particular parts of the truth of God. We, on the other hand, pay a higher regard to another part of truth. Now these various constitutions of Christians affect, in some degree, their prayers. And when they are blended they give a peculiar harmony of sweetness to the incense.

At this time it is delightful to my thoughts to think that the prayers of different nationalities are being put into the golden bowl! Our French brothers and sisters always charm me when they pray. There is a tender, filial love—an affectionate gentleness which is most delicious. Our American friends, so bold and sanguine, also delight us with their confidence in God. Their prayers will balance somewhat the timidity of the French utterance. Then, our German brethren, with their deep thoughtfulness, and their habit of going to the bottom of things—how solidly they make supplication! So with all our brothers and sisters of many lands, what a choice amalgam they make!

I have been present at prayer meetings when I have heard the various nations pray, and my heart has rejoiced, and I can conceive that to God there is a peculiar harmony in the blended prayers of the many peoples and tongues. Look back and think of the prayers of all the ages as being in the golden bowl at this one time. The prayers of the Apostles, the cries of the persecuted times, the wrestling of the lonely ones of the Middle Ages, the moans from the valleys and mountains of Piedmont—the groans of our brothers and sisters during the Marian persecution, the pleadings of Covenanters and of Puritans—all in the golden bowl together! And all with the live coals upon them, coming up from the hand of the great Covenant Angel who stands for them before the Throne, pleading with God on the behalf of His people!

Let us rejoice that the blended prayers of the Church are very sweet to the eternal God.[1] □

6

A Prayer for God's Purity

Gilbert Shaw

The pure in heart, the single eye, alone shall see my God.

O radiant Purity, that lives one fire, the fire of Love, consume me quite within Thy quenchless flame.

Thou virgin-born, Thy life, the Purity of God on earth in human frame, may we possess Thy love in purity, not for Thy gifts or favours but for Thyself alone, our all and every thought and wish and will Thine everlasting glory.

My Lord, my King, how awful is Thy Presence in the sacramental veils, the Purity of God surrendered into human hands and human guardianship.

How clean the heart should be that welcomes Thee its King, how pure the living house of prayer wherein Thou wouldst abide. How wonderfully Thou didst form that nothing but Thyself may satisfy my soul's most inward longing.

O Love, to Thee I do resign myself, let nothing of my wretched self remain but all of Thee.

I do resign myself to bear whatever Thou dost send to bear and to rejoice. For love of Thee, and in conformity to Thy good will, I now resign myself if ever it may be Thy will.

To suffer shame and slander, unearned rebuke, to be forgotten of my friends, to want for food and natural comfort, to be abandoned and ignored by all my fellow men, so that I may have none to hold to but only Thee my God.

To suffer sickness and infirmity, to die alone in a strange land and among strangers, to endure aridity and pain of soul, to follow Thee blindly, not seeking distraction or comfort in any creature, to be content to spend and to be spent for Thee.

To Thee, O Lord, I do return Thy gifts; dispose of me according to Thy will.

Let nothing cloud the mirror of my soul, Thy face alone illumine it.

Let nothing share the altar of my heart, lest strange fire, born of my unruled desire, burn thereon and cause Thee to depart.

Burn Thou alone within the temple Thou didst fashion for Thyself, and burning burn all dross of self away, so that Thou mayest ever stay and never from my life depart, that in Thy Purity I may obtain, the veil of flesh being rent by Thee, my place before the Father's Throne hid in Thy Life within all Deity. [1]

7

The Prayer Life of Jesus

Ralph I. Tilley

Years ago I was privileged to develop a relationship with a veteran preacher and Bible scholar who later became a mentor to me in many ways. We first met while serving together on a Bible college faculty, then some years later when he was serving on a local church board, he contacted me to inquire whether I would consider becoming their pastor, which I later did.

When it came to preaching on the major themes of Scripture, there was no one I enjoyed listening to more than S. I. Emery (1895-1977). He would soar in eloquence as he expounded upon the doctrine of Christ's atonement in particular. Blessed with a deep, bass voice, and preaching without a note in front of him, this dear brother's passion for Christ and the Cross was both intense and genuine. And rarely did I hear him preach, but soon into his sermon, he would have a handkerchief in hand, dabbing his nose, giving an occasional sniff, while his voice quivered as he tried to control his emotions.

As much as I enjoyed listening to Dr. Emery preach and teach the Word of God, I was blessed as well listening to him pray. He was as well-versed in the Scriptures as any person I've known, and when he prayed, he would recite appropriate Scriptures. And you could not listen to him pray but that you knew that he knew God. I loved to hear him pray. More than once while listening in on this dear brother's holy colloquy with his heavenly Father, I thought, *if I could only pray like that!*

This same desire — the desire to know God and to pray effectively — is what prompted the disciples on one occasion to say to the Master, "Lord, teach us to pray" (Luke 11:1).[1] There is no record in the Gospels of any disciple requesting that Jesus would teach the disciples how to preach or teach, though we can be certain he was a master at both. But oh . . . when the Twelve heard Jesus praying on one occasion, they were so impressed with the intimacy by which he spoke to his Father. The utter simplicity and faith with which he communed overwhelmed them. Their prayers were lifeless and listless compared to Christ's. They knew their prayer-life was sorely deficient. "Lord, teach us to pray, they pleaded.

Why Did Jesus Pray?

Jesus prayed in order to commune with his Father in Heaven. Because prayer is fundamentally communion with God (spirit communicating with Spirit), Jesus prayed so as to maintain intimate fellowship with the Father. Thus we read passages like this: "But he would often withdraw to desolate places and pray" (Luke 5:16).

Though Jesus always walked in communion and fellowship with his Father, whether in the busy marketplace, or when being grilled by his accusers, nevertheless, as the Son of Man he felt the inner need to withdraw regularly from all others. It was the call of his Father to come apart to be refreshed and renewed by his Spirit. It was the inner urge to share a private, holy, and intimate time with his Father. Their trysting times were often and precious — whether early in the morning, late at night, or in between.

Every devout Christian knows and shares a similar spiritual reality of a growing intimacy with the Father that comes from these sacred, lonely moments. Sometime before his death, the great missionary apostle to the country of China, Hudson Taylor (1832-1905), said, "The sun has never risen upon China without finding me at prayer."[2]

Jesus prayed because he wanted to know his Father's will. It is more than a textual coincidence that Luke records Jesus' praying the entire night before he chose from among all his disciples twelve men to be apostles (see Luke 6:12-16).

By the time Christ had selected these men, he had gained a following from an ever-increasing devoted group of disciples. Knowing it to be the will of the Father to choose a special group to be with him that he might reveal to them the mysteries of the Kingdom, while entrusting the future growth of his Church eventually to them, it was imperative that he call the right persons for this monumental task. Of all of the disciples who had made a commitment to follow Jesus of Nazareth, the Son of God, who should he select to serve as His apostles? It was this thought that caused him to spend an entire night in contemplation, meditation and communion with His Father: *Father, who among all of my followers should I choose to be Apostles?*

Knowing that Simon Peter would experience a tragic failure, and that Judas Iscariot would betray him, should he select these? Realizing that the Sons of Thunder, James and John, could be self-serving and self-seeking, should he take the risk in appointing them? Then there was Thomas, given to doubt and skepticism — was there any hope that he could mature and become a stable influence for righteousness? All of these thoughts, and many more, must have been cascading through the mind of Christ during the course of that night in prayer.

However, by the time the sun rose over the Judean hills the next morning, Jesus knew. He knew each man who should serve as one of his apostles. Each name had been revealed to him in prayer by his Father in Heaven.

Does not our Lord serve as the model for the Church when facing critical choices? If the Son of Man found it necessary to take an entire night in order to discern the will of his Father in selecting twelve men to be leaders, why do we think we can get by in offering a sixty-second prayer in a business meeting before we vote on who are to be our pastor and leaders? Does God still reveal his choices to praying people today? Or are we too self-assured to really care? Is God's agenda ours? Or have we taken the time to find out?

Jesus prayed because he needed to be continually filled with the Holy Spirit's power. As the second Person of the Triune God, Jesus had no need to pray — he was very God of very God, as the creed says. But as the incarnate Son of God — the Son of Man — when Jesus took upon himself human flesh, he voluntarily gave up the prerogatives of deity, thus becoming totally dependent upon his Father-God (see Phil. 2:6-7).

As a man, being completely dependent upon his heavenly Father, he was in need — as any believer is — of the Holy Spirit's power for service and ministry. At his baptism he was anointed by the Spirit for future ministry: "and he saw the Spirit of God descending like a dove and coming to rest on him" (Matt. 3:16). Jesus goes from the Jordan River — "full of the Holy Spirit" (Luke 4:1) — to be sorely tempted by Satan in the Judean wilderness. Then following the forty-days wilderness fast, Jesus "returned in the power of the Spirit to Galilee" (Luke 4:14). He then proceeds to Nazareth, where he enters his hometown synagogue, stands up and reads a passage from Isaiah, "The Spirit of the Lord is upon me" (Luke 4:18).

It is clear that Jesus needed the power of the Holy Spirit in his life and ministry. Without the Spirit, Jesus, as the Son of Man, would have been as powerless as any other man. He needed the Spirit's constant, habitual indwelling. All that the Lord Jesus Christ ever did was done in the power of the blessed Holy Spirit.

What about you and me, dear reader? Do we feel the need to be constantly refreshed, renewed and filled by the Spirit? Do we feel our need of being totally dependent on the Spirit for developing Christian character and for doing works of service? Do our daily activities reveal this need? Are we constantly lifting our hearts to the Lord for his fresh anointing and power? Or are we performing our Christian duties and ministries in the strength of the flesh and human power?

Oh, that you and I would be constantly stirred up, realizing our total dependence on the Spirit. Let us hear afresh the word of the Lord to Zerubbabel: "'Not by might, nor by power, but by my Spirit,' says the LORD of hosts" (Zech. 4:6). Just as Jesus needed the power of the Holy Spirit in life and ministry, so do we.

Join me now in praying this prayer of Elwood Stokes (1815-1895):

Thou canst fill me, gracious Spirit,
Though I cannot tell Thee how;
But I need Thee, greatly need Thee;
Come, O come and fill me now.

I am weakness, full of weakness;
At Thy sacred feet I bow.
Blest, divine, eternal Spirit,

Fill with love, and fill me now.[3]

There is a further consideration of great importance to every Christian on this topic of the prayer life of Jesus.

Why Does Jesus Pray?

What became of Jesus after he ascended into the heavens from the disciples' view some two thousand years ago? Where did Jesus go? What is he presently doing?

The Scriptures are clear: "After making purification for sins, he sat down at the right hand of the Majesty on high" (Heb. 1:3). In the language of Scripture, for the once crucified, risen Christ to be seated at the right hand of the Majesty on high, depicts a position of the highest honor and authority.

Inasmuch as the Lord Jesus Christ defeated Satan at the Cross, with the empty tomb validating this defeat, he was given a place of supreme glory and power: "Worthy is the Lamb who was slain, to receive power and wealth and wisdom and might and honor and glory and blessing!" (Rev. 5:12).

But just what is it that our triumphant Lord is doing now — this very moment in time at the Father's right hand? Hebrews 9:24 holds the answer: "For Christ has entered, not into the holy places made with hands, which are copies of the true things, but into heaven itself, now to appear in the presence of God for us." There you have it. What is our Lord and Savior engaged in at this very moment? He is in the presence of God the Father for us! While we may not be certain of the total breadth of Christ's present ministry, we do know this from revealed Scripture: he is at this very moment in Heaven in the Father's presence "for us."

The apostle Paul asks rhetorically, "Who is to condemn? Christ Jesus is the one whom died — more than that, who was raised — who is at the right hand of God, who indeed is interceding for us" (Rom. 8:34). The believing Christian may be — and often is — convicted of sin, but never condemned as a sinner. Why? Because our Mediator is interceding with the Father for us.

What does this mean? In 1 John 2:1, the apostle writes, "But if anyone does sin, we have an advocate with the Father, Jesus Christ the righteous." The Greek word "with" is full of meaning here. It means face-to-face with the Father. Here is the beautiful picture suggested: As the obedient Lamb of God, the Lord Jesus Christ offered his body and blood as the atoning sacrifice for man's sin. This he did once for all (see Heb. 9:28). But as the risen, triumphant Lord, he took his five wounds to Heaven with him. Christ still bears the scars of the Cross: "there is one mediator between God and men, the man Christ Jesus" (1 Tim. 2:5).

The glorious fact is, that whenever a Christian fails in his walk with God (which he often does), he need not despair; he has an Advocate and Intercessor who shows the Father his wounds — wounds the Lamb still bears because his people desperately need an ever-interceding Advocate as well as a Savior. Charles Wesley (1707-1788) said it well:

> *Arise, my soul, arise.*
> *Shake off thy guilty fears.*
> *The bleeding sacrifice*
> *In my behalf appears.*
> *Before the throne my Surety stands,*
> *Before the throne my Surety stands;*
> *My name is written on His hands.*
>
> *Five bleeding wounds He bears,*
> *Received on Calvary.*
> *They pour effectual prayers;*
> *They strongly plead for me.*
> *Forgive him, oh, forgive, they cry.*
> *Forgive him, oh forgive, they cry,*
> *Nor let that ransomed sinner die.*[4]

It is the sacrificial offering of Christ's blood on the Cross that redeems us; it is Christ's present intercessions at the Majesty's right hand that preserves us.

Dear reader, I have had some wonderful godly people through the years to pray for me, and as I mentioned at the beginning of this article, I have enjoyed and been moved to the depths of my soul while listening to the prayers of some of God's choicest saints. But to know there is One in the presence of my Father just now interceding for Ralph I. Tilley provides me with the greatest assurance and hope. What about you?

You will recall that one day during our Lord's earthly ministry he took the self-assured Simon Peter aside. He knew how spiritually fragile the apostle was, though Peter himself did not. Jesus tenderly confided in Peter, "Simon, Simon, behold Satan demanded to have you, that he might sift you as wheat. but I have prayed for you that your faith may not fail" (Luke 22:31-32). As we know, Simon Peter did go on to deny the Lord Jesus Christ. But he repented, later was filled with the Holy Spirit, and went on to become one of the church's strong pillars. It would never have happened without the prayers of Jesus.

Robert Murray M'Cheyne (1813-1843) once said, "If I could hear Christ praying for me in the next room I would not fear a million enemies. Yet distance makes no difference. He is praying for me."[5]

Prayer: *Lord, even as your disciples implored you to teach them to pray, so would I. And while I make this request, I would at the same time give you thanks, O Christ, thanks for interceding for me and your Church — now and forever at the Father's right hand. Amen.*

8

The Praying Plumber of Lisburn

A. W. Tozer

Y ou have only to glance at his round red face and his twinkling blue eyes to guess the place of his birth. And when he smiles and says, "Guid marnin," there is no doubt left Tom Haire is Irish.

It is not with Tom Haire the Irishman that we are concerned here, however, but with Brother Tom Haire, the servant of Christ. So fully has he lost himself in God that the text "not I, but Christ," actually seems to be a reality in his life. I think I have never heard him quote the text, but his whole being is a living exemplification of it. He appears to live the text each moment of each day.

Tom Haire was born sixty-six years ago in County Down, North Ireland ("Protestant Ireland," as Tom always carefully explains), and apart from two visits to the United States has lived all his life there. He is a member of the Episcopal Church of Ireland, the "disestablished" wing of the Episcopal Church whose worship is much simpler and less ornate than that of the Anglicans and which is evangelical in belief and evangelistic in spirit. He is a lay preacher and evangelist, but until recently stayed very close to Lisburn, his home, where his plumbing business is located. He was so busy with his business and his evangelistic work, he says with a twinkle, that he did not get around to finding a wife till he was thirty-nine years old. He has a married daughter, Margaret, whose husband now looks after Tom's business affairs. His wife has been dead for thirteen years.

The two characteristics that mark Tom Haire as unusual are his utter devotion to prayer and his amazing spiritual penetration. (And are not the two always closely associated?) Three months after his conversion, when he was sixteen years old, he formed the habit of praying four hours each day. This practice he followed faithfully for many years. Later he added one all-night prayer session each week. In 1930 these weekly all-night prayer times were increased to two, and in 1943 he settled down to the habit of praying three nights of every week. He gets along on very little sleep. In addition to the three nights each week that he stays awake to pray, he is frequently awakened in the night seasons by a passage of Scripture or a burden of prayer that will not let him rest. "And almost always," he says, "the Lord wakens me early in the morning to pray."

Tom Haire is a rare compound of deep, tender devotion, amazing good sense and a delightful sense of humor. There is about him absolutely nothing of the tension found in so many persons who seek to live the spiritual life.

Tom is completely free in the Spirit and will not allow himself to be brought under bondage to the rudiments of the world nor the consciences of other people. His attitude toward everyone and everything is one of good-natured tolerance if he does not like it, or smiling approval if he does. The things he does not like he is sure to pray about, and the things he approves he is sure to make matters of thanksgiving to God. But always he is relaxed and free from strain. He will not allow himself to get righteously upset about anything. "I lie near to the heart of God, he says, and I fear nothing in the world."

That he lies near to God's heart is more than a passing notion to Tom. It is all very real and practical. "God opens His heart," he says, "and takes us in. In God all things are beneath our feet. All power is given to us and we share God's almightiness." He has no confidence at all in mankind, but believes that God must be all in all. Not even our loftiest human desires or holiest prayers are acceptable to God. "The river flows from beneath the throne," he explains, "and its source is not of this world. So the source of our prayers must be Christ Himself hidden in our hearts."

Though he counts heavily on the power of prayer he has no faith in the virtue of prayer itself as such. He warns against what he calls merit-prayer, by which he means any prayer offered with the secret notion that there is something good in it which will impress God and which He must recognize and reward. Along with "merit-prayer" goes "merit-faith," which is the faith we think will in some way please God.

"Too many of God's people are straining for faith," says Tom, "and holding on hard trying to exercise it. This will never do at all. The flesh cannot believe no matter how hard it tries, and we only wear ourselves out with our human efforts. True faith is the gift of God to an obedient soul and comes of itself without effort. The source of faith is Christ in us. It is a fruit of the Spirit."

He flatly rejects the notion that we "can buy something with prayer." "God's gifts come from another source," he insists. "They are 'freely given,' and have no price attached. It is the goodness of God that gives us all things. God gives His free gifts generously to those of His children who bring themselves into harmony with His will. Then they have but to ask and He gives."

Brother Tom fasts quite often and sometimes the fast is prolonged for some time. But he scorns the thought that there is any merit in it. "Some people," says Tom with a shake of the head, "some people half kill themselves by ascetic practices. They imagine God to be so severe that He enjoys seeing them hungry. They go about pale and weak in the mistaken belief that they are making themselves dear to God. All such notions come from the flesh and are false." Once during a prolonged season of prayer he got suddenly thirsty and without a qualm of conscience broke off prayer and went out for a cup of tea. This got him into difficulties with certain fellow Christians who felt that he was surrendering to fleshly appetites. But he has dwelt so long in the spacious heart of God that he is unaffected by the scruples of others. God's heart is no strait jacket even if some imperfectly taught saints insist on acting as if it were. "Where the Spirit of the Lord is, there is liberty."

Wherever there is a strain in the life we may be sure the flesh is operating. The Holy Spirit gives fruitful burdens but never brings strain. Our very eagerness to have our prayers answered may cause us to lapse into the flesh if we are not watchful. So Tom reasons. A woman sent for him recently and wanted him to pray for her healing. She was in very bad condition, but Tom would not pray. He detected in her eagerness to get well a bit of rebellion against the will of God. So he set about breaking her rebellion down. "Sister," he asked innocently, "and have you ever read the Scripture, 'Precious in the sight of the Lord is the death of his saints'? Sure, and you would not want to rob the Lord of all that preciousness, would you?" It was his way of telling her that she was not fit to live unless she was willing to die. The shock had its intended effect, and after some further conversation Tom felt that the woman had surrendered her will to God. Then he prayed for her healing. She received some help physically, and in addition she had also the benefit that comes from a new spiritual experience.

Tom holds back from the highly advertised healing meeting, but he ardently believes that an outpouring of the Holy Spirit on a life may easily result in physical healing. "Should God ever pour out His Spirit again upon all flesh," he says, "we may expect physical healings to accompany the outpouring. It is part of the divine pattern."

Tom's conception of prayer is so lofty and so different from the popular conception as to be something of another order entirely. To him, prayer is a spiritual art, subject to divine laws which must be obeyed if our prayers are to achieve success. "Harmony" and "dominion" are two words that come easily from his lips when talking about prayer.

Once in a sermon I spoke of God's making man in His image. At the close of the service Tom spoke a word of approval of the sermon and then went on to develop the thought further. He called attention to the words occurring so close together, "image" and "dominion." "Do you notice," he asked, "how God made man in His own image and then gave him dominion? The dominion followed the image, and so it is with us now. Our dominion in prayer depends upon how much of the image of God we carry in our hearts. There must be complete harmony between the soul and God if we are to enjoy answered prayer. The degree of success we enjoy in prayer depends upon the image within us." Then he added a significant sentence: "For instance, God would not hear a man who would kick a dog."

It was four o'clock of a bitterly cold November morning when the telephone rang and an excited voice told me that the Norwood Hotel was burning and the guests were fleeing into the street in their night clothes to escape the flames.

Leonard Ravenhill, the English evangelist, and his prayer helper, Tom Haire, who were engaged in evangelistic meetings in our local church, were staying at the Norwood. My informant could tell me nothing about these men. He only knew that some guests had died in the fire and others had been badly injured.

In a few minutes one of the elders of the church picked me up and together we raced over the icy streets to the scene of the fire. The police and firemen had the area blocked off. The basement of the First Nazarene Church, located within one block of the hotel, had been converted into a first-aid station and the less seriously injured victims of the fire were being cared for there. A hurried search among the shivering and frightened persons who had gathered in the church basement failed to discover either Ravenhill or Haire. The excited guests could not tell us anything about them, but some thought that the two men had been among the victims who had jumped from the hotel windows.

The next logical place to look was St. Bernard Hospital, a few blocks away. There the scene was one of confusion. We stopped one of the hurrying sisters and inquired whether two Protestant evangelists had been admitted to the hospital in the last few minutes. The sister replied that she did not know. "But," she added, "as I helped to bring in one elderly man who had been hurt in the fire, he patted my cheek and asked me if I loved Jesus." We did not need to ask further. We had found Tom.

Both Mr. Ravenhill and Mr. Haire had been seriously injured by the long jump to the pavement from the third story window of the hotel, Both had broken bones in many parts of their bodies. Tom suffered deep burns on one hand and Ravenhill received internal injuries.

Nothing else within the sphere of my own experience has demonstrated so beautifully the real quality of present-day Christians as did the hotel accident suffered by the two evangelists. The news wires carried the story to every part of the United States and Canada and finally to England and Ireland. Immediately telegrams and long distance calls began to flood in to my office from far parts of the continent. Churches wrote to offer assistance; Christian nurses and doctors volunteered their aid; visitors came in great numbers and prayer went up like incense from coast to coast. The two men hovered for a while between life and death and then slowly began to get well.

Whatever cynical unbelief may say, there are many persons who believe that the multitude of intercessions made for others were returning on the heads of God's servants. For everyone who says, "Why did this happen to praying men?" there are others who exclaim, "How could mortal man come through all this and still live?" By every natural evidence they should have died. That they are alive today is due to the kindness of God and the determined prayers of God's people.

The weeks spent in St. Bernard Hospital revealed the workings of God in many ways. It was not long before the news had spread through the hospital that a Protestant "saint" had come among them. Nurses, doctors, supervisors and "sisters" of various kinds came to see Tom for themselves. Some of them admitted that they had not been aware that such men as Tom were still to be found running loose. Though their teachings forbade them to believe that Tom was a real Christian, their yearning hearts were better and more charitable than their dogmas, and they soon accepted him not as a Christian only but as a superior saint who could teach them the things of the Spirit.

Among those who visited Tom was a distinguished professor of philosophy at Notre Dame University. He came not to try to convert Tom but to hear from his mouth the wonders of a life of prayer and worship. In the course of his conversations he admitted that he was very much dissatisfied with the kind of Christian being produced within the Catholic fold. "They come to me and confess their sins," he said, "and then go back and do the same things again. I do not believe in that kind of religion. When a man comes to Christ he should come with John the Baptist repentance." This may sound trite to the average evangelical, but coming from a highly placed prelate of the Roman Church it is little less than astounding. And the whole experience suggests that there may be many others enmeshed in the toils of Romanism who would look our way if we presented more examples of true godliness to catch their attention.

Tom's experience in the hospital was not without humorous incidents, though Tom was extremely careful never to give offense to the Catholic personnel. One Friday he suddenly developed an appetite for meat and called a nurse to him. "I say," suster, he began, "I crave a wee piece o'roast chucken. D'ye suppose ye cud get me some?" The nurse said No. It was Friday, and besides, chicken was not served to patients in that hospital. That was final. "But," Tom persisted, "But, suster. Ye don't know who I am! Tomorrah the British consul is comin' to see me.

And besides that, look at the green light above me bed, put there in honor of auld Ireland. Now do I get some chucken?" Tom's blue eyes were twinkling. The consul's visit was scarcely to be in honor of Tom, and the green light above the bed surely had no remote relation to Tom's birthplace. The nurse left the room shaking her head doubtfully. After a while she reappeared all smiles, and on a tray she carried a plate laden with roast chicken. Tom ate the meal with relish. He undoubtedly enjoyed it, but more than all he enjoyed the fact that he had gotten roast chicken in a Catholic hospital on Friday.

One day as a supervisor was in his room, Tom suddenly asked her to pray for him. She promised she would go immediately to the chapel and say a prayer for him. But that would not do. "No," Tom insisted, "I want you to pray for me now. Right here." The surprised sister scrambled around in her voluminous bag and came up with a prayer book out of which she read a prayer. Then to be sure she would not leave, Tom grabbed her hand and hung on. "Now, suster, I'll pray for you." Then he launched into one of his tender, impassioned prayers while the sister stood reverently with bowed head. When he was through there was awe in her voice as she said, "That wasn't a memorized prayer, was it, Tom? That came right out of your heart. The Holy Ghost must have given you that." Until the day breaks and the shadows flee away it will not be revealed how much was accomplished through the suffering man of God by such faithful witnessing among persons who for all their blindness are at least reverent and serious-minded.

When the men were recovered sufficiently to be moved, a United States Army ambulance plane flew them to New York where they were the guests of the army for one day. Then they were flown overseas to their respective homes in England and Ireland.

While Tom was going through the long siege of suffering after his accident, he was forced for the first time in years to give up his habit of praying three nights each week. He missed having these long seasons of intercession, but he did not let it bother him nor did he allow himself to get under bondage because he could not pray as before. God knew that His servant would be back at his regular habit as soon as he could, and Tom knew that He knew and understood. Between friends there are some things that can be taken for granted.

One day not long ago Tom came shuffling into the church, his face shining a bit more than usual and his voice full of excitement like a boy that had just received a sled or a pony for his birthday. The reason for his new joy was that God had enabled him to go back to his old habit of all-night prayer again! He feels so much "butter," he says, that he can stay up all night now without any trouble.

But Tom will probably never again be able to kneel before God as he had been doing for fifty years. The crushed pelvis and the broken back are "butter," it is true, but they will not permit him to bend very much at best. He must now do his praying sitting up for the most part, though when be is by himself he often stretches full length on the floor as he goes over his long prayer lists or worships the Lord in the beauty of holiness. I have come upon him sometimes lying prone before the Lord quietly wrestling against the evil one whom he calls "Seten." And so completely free is he that when he is interrupted in prayer by the unexpected entrance of a friend, he simply breaks off his praying, scrambles to his feet and enters into a relaxed and delightful conversation about anything that the visitor may have on his mind. Tom will talk about anything, but he is never so keen nor so original as when talking about the goodness of God and the power of prayer.

The doctors have told Tom that his accident has probably prolonged his life many years by forcing a long rest just at the period in his life when his heart stood in need of it. Of course such a matter is in the hand of God and any prediction of longevity would be altogether rash and foolhardy. But one thing is sure: whether he stays among us for many years or slips off to Heaven tomorrow is not of any consequence to Tom. He has lived so long on the portico of Heaven that he will feel quite at home when the Father comes out and invites him inside.[1] ☐

9

Will and Emotions

J. Sidlow Baxter

When I entered the ministry in 1928, I determined that I would be the most Methodist Baptist in the history of the world. Talk about perfectionism! Talk about making plans for the day! They must have been a marvel to both angels and demons.

But, just as the stars in their courses fought against Sisera long ago, so the stars in their courses seemed set on smashing my well-made plans to smithereens. Oh, I would start. You know, I'd rise at 5:30. Fifteen minutes to wash and dress. Then an hour and a half of prayer and Bible reading. Half an hour for breakfast. Thirty minutes for a constitutional—to walk up to the woods, breathe deep and, when nobody was looking, run now and again—that's a constitutional.

Now, I won't take time telling you all the subtle subterfuges which Satan used to trip me up and trick me out of keeping my plans. But I found that with increasing administrative duties and responsibilities in the pastorate, my plans were going haywire. My time for prayer was getting crowded out and my periods of study with the Bible were getting scarcer.

That was bad enough, but it was worse when I began to get used to it. And then I began excusing myself. My prayer life became a case of sinning and repenting. Every time I got down to pray I had to start weeping and asking the Lord's forgiveness. I had to repent that I hadn't prayed more and ask him to help me to do better in the future. All such things really take the pleasure out of praying!

A Crisis

Then it all came to a crisis. At a certain time one morning I looked at my watch. According to my plan, for I was still bravely persevering, I was to withdraw for an hour of prayer.

I looked at my watch and it said: "Time for prayer, Sid." But I looked at my desk and there was a miniature mountain of correspondence. And Conscience said, "You ought to answer those letters." So, as we say in Scotland, I swithered (doubt, waver). Shall it be prayer? Shall it be letters? Prayer? Letters? Yes, no. Yes, no. And while I was swithering, a velvety little voice began to speak in my inner consciousness: "Look here, Sid, what's all this bother? You know very well what you should do. The practical thing is to get those letters answered. You can't afford the time for prayer this morning. Get those letters answered."

But I still swithered, and the voice began to reinforce what it had said.

It said, "Look here, Sid, don't you think the Lord knows all the busy occupations which are taking your time? You're converted, you're born again, and you're in the ministry. People are crowding in; you're having conversions. Doesn't that show that God is pleased with you? And even if you can't pray, don't worry too much about you. Look Sid, you'd better face up to it. You're not one of the spiritual ones."

I don't want to use extravagant phrases, but if you had plunged a dagger into my bosom it couldn't have hurt me more. "Sid, you are not one of the spiritual ones."

I'm not the introspective type, but that morning I took a good look into Sidlow Baxter. And I found that there was an area of me that did not want to pray. I had to admit it.

A Battle

I didn't want to pray. But I looked more closely and I found that there was a part of me that did. The part that didn't was the emotions, and the part that did was the intellect and the will.

Suddenly I found myself asking Sidlow Baxter: "Are you going to let your will be dragged about by your changeful emotions?" And I said to my will: "Will, are you ready for prayer?" And Will said, "Here I am, I'm ready." So I said, "Come on, Will, we will go."

So Will and I set off to pray. But the minute we turned our footsteps to go and pray, all my emotions began to talk: "We're not coming, we're not coming, we're not coming." And I said to Will, "Will, can you stick to it?" And Will said, "Yes, if you can." So Will and I, we dragged off those wretched emotions and we went to pray, and stayed an hour in prayer.

If you had asked me afterwards, "Did you have a good time?" do you think I could have said yes? A good time? No, it was a fight all the way!

What I would have done without the companionship of Will, I don't know. In the middle of the most earnest intercession, I suddenly found one of the principal emotions way out on the golf course, playing golf. And I had to run to the golf course and say, "Come back." And a few minutes later I found another of the emotions; it had traveled one and a half days in advance and it was in the pulpit preaching a sermon I had not even yet prepared. And I had to say, "Come back."

I certainly couldn't have said we had a good time. It was exhausting, but we did it. The next morning came. I looked at my watch and it was time. I said to Will, "Come on, Will, it's time for prayer."

And all the emotions began to pull the other way, and I said "Will, can you stick to it?" And Will said, "Yes, in fact I think I'm stronger after the struggle yesterday morning." So Will and I went in again.

The same thing happened. Rebellious, tumultuous, uncooperative emotions. If you had asked me, "Have you had a good time?" I would have had to tell you with tears, No, the heavens were like brass. It was a job to concentrate. I had an awful time with the emotions."

A Victory

This went on for about two and a half weeks. But Will and I stuck it out. Then one morning during that third week, I looked at my watch and I said, "Will, it's time for prayer. Are you ready?" And Will said, "Yes, I'm ready."

And just as we were going in I heard one of my chief emotions say to the others. "Come on, fellows, there's no use wearing ourselves out; they'll go on whatever we do."

That morning we didn't have any hilarious experience or wonderful visions with heavenly voices and raptures. But Will and I were able, with less distraction, to get on with praying. And that went on for another two or three weeks. In fact, Will and I had begun to forget the emotions. I would say, "Will, are you ready for prayer?" And Will replied, "Yes, I'm always ready."

Suddenly one day while Will and I were pressing our case at the throne of the heavenly glory, one of the chief emotions shouted, "Hallelujah!" and all the other emotions suddenly shouted, "Amen!" For the first time the whole territory of James Sidlow Baxter was happily coordinated in the exercises of prayer, and God suddenly became real and Heaven was wide open and Christ was there and the Holy Spirit was moving and I knew that all the time, God had been listening.

The point is this: the validity and the effectuality of prayer are not determined or even affected by the subjective psychological condition of the one who prays. The thing that makes prayer valid and vital and moving and operative is "My FAITH takes hold of God's truth."

Brothers and sisters, soon now, we shall be meeting him. When you meet him, and I speak reverently, when you feel his arms around you, and when you embrace as well as adore him, don't you want to be able to look into that wonderful face and say, "Lord, at last I'm seeing face-to-face the One I have for years known heart to heart."

Why don't you resolve that from this time on, you will be a praying Christian? You will never, never, never regret it! NEVER!!![1]

10

Submission

William Cowper

O Lord, my best desire fulfil,
And help me to resign
Life, health, and comfort to Thy will,
And make Thy pleasure mine.

Why would I shrink at Thy command,
Whose love forbids my fears?
Or tremble at the gracious hand
That wipes away my tears?

No, rather let me freely yield
What most I prize to Thee;
Who never hast a good withheld,
Or wilt withhold, from me.

Thy favor, all my journey through,
Thou art engaged to grant;
What else I want, or think I do,
'Tis better still to want.

Wisdom and mercy guide my way,

Shall I resist them both?
A poor blind creature of day,
And crush'd before the moth!

But ah! my inward spirit cries,
Still binds me to Thy sway;
Else the next cloud that veils the skies
Drives all these thoughts away.[1]

11

Bending Low in Prayer

Ralph I. Tilley

Those who are intimately acquainted with spiritual realities, know that just as there are seasons in the natural world, so there are seasons of the soul. As I write this, here on the North American continent, autumn has officially begun. Even now as I glance up from my keyboard, I can look out my study window and see the early morning sun highlighting varying shades of greens and yellows on the poplars in our back yard. Fall is here; nature is once again entering her cycle of decay, dormancy, and death.

While there are inevitable natural cycles of the soul—seasons of remarkable growth as well as periods of apparent fruitlessness—what is unnatural and unacceptable, are seasons of sin—lukewarmness, disobedience, and a loss of our first love.

Whenever the Christian has become careless in his walk with God, thereby grieving the Holy Spirit because of his carelessness, failure, and sin, or has slowly lost his passion for Christ and the things of God, the faithful Spirit calls us to confession and repentance. It requires bending low before the Lord.

Ted Rendall writes, "Individually, this brokenness before God will mean a new honesty that admits the lack of daily Bible reading, meaningful prayer, and measurable growth in the Christian life." He goes on to say, "It may mean a conquest over the tyranny of television, the spell of sports, and the passion of possessions."[1]

Corporately, when we bend low before the Lord in deep repentance, steps will be taken to correct wrongs. Where fractured relationships have occurred in the body of Christ, a convicted Christian will take measures to heal that relationship. Where a board member, elder, or deacon has manifested in a committee meeting an un-Christlike spirit, he will leave no stone unturned until he has apologized and asked the brothers to forgive him. Where there has been a clear lack of faithfulness in fulfilling one's ministry responsibilities, the repentant believer will acknowledge such to those he is responsible to and correct his ways.

Our Desperate Need

Where there are dry eyes, a lack of conversions, rigid ritualism, frigid formalism, rampant materialism, sterile intellectualism, passionless preaching, predictable prayer meetings, failing marriages, rebellious teens, secret sinning, faithless leaders — *there* is the need for a Heaven-sent revival. REVIVAL!

Looking around a land that had once been favored by God with untold blessings, but had since fallen into idolatry, breaking her covenant with the Lord, the psalmist cries out, "Will you not revive us again? (Psa. 85:6).[2]

The word "revive" comes from a combination of Latin words and means to "live again." We use this term in a number of ways. For example, the person who has experienced cardiac arrest, but was blessed to have medical technicians come to his aid with a defibrillator, was suddenly revived — caused to live again.

It pains me to say this, but all perceptive believers know it to be true — a multitude of Christians, local churches, and ministries are either dead or dying and are in desperate need of a Heaven-sent revival. Pastors must lead the way. Pastors must be revived themselves if they are to see their church revived. Oh, I realize some churches will never experience a genuine resurrection — even with a Spirit-filled pastor, but those churches are exceptions. God's usual way is to work through the church's leaders, the ministry's leaders.

During the widespread Canadian revival, which began in the early 1970s, scores of ministers were revived by the Spirit of God as well as parishioners. The late Kurt Koch (1913-1987) recorded many of these accounts. For example, he writes, "While Pastor McLeod was preaching in a certain church, another minister, who was sitting in the congregation, interrupted and said, 'Stop for a moment. I am on my way to hell if I do not at once confess my sin and accept the Lord Jesus.'" Bill stopped in the middle of his sermon. The minister came forward and openly confessed his sins.

Dr. Koch tells of another minister. He was a man who claimed to have received the baptism of the Holy Spirit. Under the preaching of an evangelist, he broke down despite all his pride. He came out and confessed his sin. Koch reports, "When he went home, his wife and children were amazed at the change that had come over him. He had been a father whose outbursts of rage had terrified the members of his family for years. Now this devout wolf had become a lamb." On another occasion, "A minister who had been trained at university was touched by the Spirit of the revival. His whole past came back before his eyes, and terrified him. He could find no peace until he had informed the university that he had cheated in his final examination and thus gained the diploma by false pretense."[3] (It should be noted, as Dr. Koch does, private sins should be confessed privately, and public sins should be confessed publicly.)

The Proven Path

Prior to crying out to God for a much-needed revival, the psalmist first reflected upon the previous mercies the Lord had shown to Israel: "LORD, you were favorable to your land; you restored the fortunes of Jacob. You forgave the iniquity of your people; you covered all their sin" (Psa. 85:1-2).

For those who have experienced better days — days of blessing and spiritual growth, days of jubilance and joy, days of purity and power, days of fellowship and fruitfulness, days of passion and productivity, days of faithfulness and fullness, days of intimacy with Christ and intercessions for others — days that are now but a dim memory, take courage — you can live again, if you really want to.

Yes, my thirsty-hearted friend, you can be forgiven and renewed. You can live again — really live!

Passionate Praying

The psalmist craved to see change — to see hearts changed, to see faces change, to see the joy of the Lord return to his people once again. He pled, "Restore us again, O God of our salvation. . . . Show us your steadfast love, O LORD . . ." (Psa. 85:4, 7).

What an expression of holy discontentment! This true child of Abraham was aroused, stirred, disturbed, and restless — prerequisites for personal and corporate revival. He was praying for revival; he even wrote his prayer down that it might be recited in the hearing of his fellow worshipers. Now, centuries later, the Spirit is still using this prayer to stir up God's people.

Are you praying for revival — in your own heart, in your local church, in your ministry? Seriously praying? Charles Spurgeon (1834-1892) wrote that when God wants to perform a new work in the hearts and lives of his people, he first sets his own people to praying.

In relating his account of the Spirit's deep move on the Asbury College campus in 1970, a revival that spread within six months to at least 130 colleges and seminaries, as well as scores of churches, Dr. Harold Spann noted, "If the full story were ever to be known, doubtless there were hundreds, if not thousands, of burdened people . . . around the world on their knees pleading for Asbury. The same could be said of every other place that has known great revival. They will never be known on this earth, but their prayers have been heard in Heaven."[4]

There is no other way to revival than the way of prayer. Not that we can *cause* revival. No! We can't cause revival. But we can position ourselves to be a channel of grace, a channel through which the Spirit of intercession himself can pray through us — even with "groanings too deep for words" (Rom. 8:26).

A Personal Covenant

Don't be surprised if your prayers for new life become personal — praying for yourself — so personal that you may be led to make a covenant. Following his reflections upon Israel's past blessings, and his pleadings for God to reveal himself once again in power and glory, the psalmist makes a personal commitment and covenant: "Let me hear what God the LORD will speak, for he will speak peace to his people, to his saints" (Psa. 85:8).

Here is one of the open secrets to personal revival — listening to what the Lord has to say to *me*. This is not only the secret to revival, this is the secret to spiritual *survival*—listening to God.

The psalmist covenanted with God to listen. Recently, while in meditation and prayer for a deeper work of God in my own life and in the life of the church where I pastor, I was led by the Lord to begin something new. Ever since I first came to Christ, in addition to a morning devotional time, I have always prayed before going to sleep — however, not always on my knees. But I was recently drawn by the Lord to spend some time on my knees before retiring for the night, praying for a fresh move of his Spirit upon my own heart, and for a mighty work of his Spirit among our local fellowship of believers. By the grace of God, I am joining with the psalmist when he said, "Let me hear what God the LORD will speak."

Are there those reading these words who will join with me? Will you go to your knees and beseech the Lord to visit you with fresh fire? Will you pray for a powerful move of the Spirit upon the heart of your pastor? Will you pray that God would be pleased to "rend the heavens and come down" (Isa. 64:1) — in your church? Will you covenant to hear what God the LORD will say? To pray earnestly. To pray faithfully.

It Need Not Take Years

Being sovereign, God is free to act in revival blessing whenever and however he chooses. There are times when God chooses to withhold the rains; then, there are times when God chooses to open the windows of Heaven. While God is sovereign, within his sovereignty he usually chooses to work through his divinely appointed means. Prayer is one of those means, fasting is another. Other means are conducting special services for the promotion of revival, reading his Word, and reading good books about how God has worked in the lives of his people in revival power.

I was recently stirred as I read an account from the life of James A. Stewart (1896-1990), the Scottish evangelist, now with the Lord. Stewart wrote:

> One day in a northern city of Eastern Europe I was concerned because, for no apparent reason, God had suddenly sent revival. In other cities and countries it usually comes after several weeks or even months of throne ministry. But here on the

fifth day, the heavens were rent asunder, and we were deluged with Heaven-sent blessing. One thousand believers packed the church building each morning for Bible study. Thousands heard the Gospel in the evening in a larger auditorium. So great was the hunger for the Word among the unsaved that there was no room for the believers in the evening service. I asked them to go to their own churches and pray and not take up the seats which should be occupied with the unsaved. The spiritual distress among the unsaved was great, as the Sword of the Spirit stabbed their hearts night after night. It was midnight and after before I could leave the building.

I was greatly disturbed in my mind and could not sleep, being at a loss to explain the open windows (Mal. 3:10). I had arrived unheralded and unknown, only by the invitation of the Holy Spirit. The meetings had commenced on a Friday night with some seven people at a prayer meeting.

One evening the Lord very kindly allowed me to discover the secret of the blessing. Being afraid that I would not have sufficient power of the Holy Spirit to proclaim the Gospel to the thousands who had gathered, I made my way to the basement of the auditorium in order to have a few minutes more of prayer. I began to pray in the darkness, but it was not long before I felt an overwhelming sense of the majesty of God. I knew right away there was someone else in the large basement, praying. I quietly put on the light, and there I saw at the extreme end of the basement some twelve sisters, flat on their faces before God! They were totally unaware of my presence. They were inside the veil, touching the Throne, by the power of the Spirit, while upstairs God was working mightily among the unsaved.[5]

Will We Obey?

If we are to see fresh moves of the Spirit in the church and in our own life, it takes more than prayer, of course; it requires obedience. The psalmist alludes to this in different ways: "let them not turn back to folly . . . faithfulness springs up from the ground . . . Righteousness will go before him and make his footsteps a way" (Psa. 85:8, 11, 13).

Are we willing to abandon our foolish ways? Will we allow God to perform a deep work of grace in us until we are faithful to him and his church? Are you ready to live anew? Let us bend low in prayer.

12

Whatever Happened to the Prayer Meeting

George Verwer

S amuel Chadwick (1860-1932), one of God's great men of past years, taught that Satan's greatest aim is to destroy our prayer lives. Satan is not afraid of prayerless study, prayerless work or prayerless religion—but he will tremble when we pray. If Chadwick was correct (and many other great men of God have said similar things), then we have a problem. If there is any part of our church life that seems to be in trouble, it is the prayer meeting. In fact, in an increasing number of churches, for all practical purposes, there is no such meeting at all.

There is no lack of books on prayer, and most pastors preach on prayer every now and again. But if there is any doctrine to which we pay only lip service in our churches, it has to be the doctrine of prayer. I have ministered in thousands of churches over the past twenty-two years in Europe, North America and around the world and I have never ceased to be amazed at the neglect of true, heart-felt, corporate prayer. There are some beautiful exceptions, of course, but they are few by comparison. I sometimes wonder whether another challenge or message on prayer will do any good. The hour has come for us to pray. Let us put the prayer meeting back into the life of our churches.

Part of my motivation for writing this article came after a weekend of ministry in a church where the midweek prayer meeting had been dropped, due mainly to lack of interest and attendance. The Holy Spirit worked during that weekend, and in the final meeting on Sunday evening the pastor announced that they would start the prayer meeting again on the following Wednesday evening. Later, I heard that some fifty people had attended and that they had a great time of prayer. The fact that some churches do have good, lively, powerful prayer meetings even in this activistic, leisure-loving, television age is proof that your church can do so as well. But it will take action, discipline and perseverance, combined with large amounts of love, patience and spiritual reality.

Some Christians tell me that they have stopped going to dead, badly organized prayer meetings, while others continue only from a sense of duty or guilt. Should we not be drawn into the presence of the living God with higher motivation than this? Why are we attracted only by special speakers and programs, rather than to the Lord himself? What real authority does the Lord Jesus have in our churches today? What authority does he have in your life and mine if we do not give top priority to meeting regularly with his people to pray?

The Need for Change

To see things change will take both a spiritual and practical revolution. We need a divine combination of practical change and deeper commitment. Pastors spend hours preparing for a sermon, but how much time is put into preparing for the prayer meeting? Linked with this is the great compromise of changing the prayer meeting to a midweek service or "prayer and Bible study" that involves only ten to twenty minutes of actual intercession after the Bible study and prayer requests. I suppose some feel this is better than nothing, but many decide that "nothing" is better and so they just don't attend.

Some really lively churches with which I have contact, have prayer and Bible study on separate nights in order to give enough time for both. Others have them together, but make the meeting long enough to include at least one hour of prayer. Some hold prayer meetings in various homes, which is good, although often on these occasions there is a tendency for there to be more fellowship than prayer. And when these groups do pray, they often seem to lack reality in the area of intercession.

These functions should not take the place of at least one good church prayer meeting each week at which a large part of the congregation meets. We should follow the example we find in Acts 1:14, "They all joined together constantly in prayer."

The lack and neglect of such meetings is, I believe, one of the greatest mistakes in our Bible-believing churches, and such deception by Satan represents a far greater enemy than liberal theology or the cults. In fact, a clear study of 2 Corinthians 10:4-7 would show us that prayer is the principal means through which we are going to stand against the enemy whatever way he might attack us. We seem to be blind to the nature of spiritual warfare and feel that as long as we have a full Sunday school and good numbers on Sunday morning then all is well. Could it be true that if the Holy Spirit left us, very few changes would be made? Would everything go on as usual?

We should be willing to do almost anything to keep from such a deadly state. It seems to be almost too late in some places, where spiritual schizophrenia has set in at such a deep level. This will be changed only by radical, deep-rooted repentance. Surely the prayer meeting, and our personal prayer lives, must be of vital importance if anything lasting and real is to take place at the center of church life. Let us put Christ back into his rightful place as Lord of our own lives and of our church programs.

Church Leaders Must Act

The responsibility for action rests with pastors and church leaders, with a need for the cooperation of every church member. It is vital that church leaders meet together for discussion and prayer on specific action they should take to make the prayer meeting a main event in their churches. Pastors need to realize the importance of firm preaching and teaching on the biblical basis for prayer. They also need to point out some of the things to avoid in prayer meetings; praying too long at one time, preaching at others in our prayers, praying only for the needs of our own church, not changing anything from week to week, judging and looking down on people who pray differently or who lack ability in English or theology, and not really believing or expecting any answers. A lot of good books on prayer are now available and should be widely distributed among the congregation, along with other informative books such as Operation World. Church leaders should wait on

God and prepare in a serious way so that each prayer meeting is carefully planned and fully used.

Conducting the Prayer Meeting

As far as the prayer meeting itself is concerned, how can we actively get out of the rut which often makes this the most boring, unpopular meeting of the week? I'd like to pass on a few suggestions used effectively for more than twenty years in our work. We have discovered that to vary the format of the meeting is extremely important, as the more accustomed we become to routines, the less vital it is to us. It can be varied by sometimes beginning with worship, intercession and thanksgiving; other times with a brief challenge to prayer. If ministry from the Word is given it should be short and yet powerful; individuals could also share specific answers to prayer.

Prayer must involve the mind as well as the heart, and long periods that do not require personal involvement allow the mind to drift. Therefore, it is good to break into groups so that each person is given the opportunity to participate. Each group could, for example, be given information about one area of need and be asked to concentrate their prayers on that.

We use films, videos and filmstrips whenever possible and applicable. Many mission groups have produced some very effective ones that are a good stimulus to prayer. When showing slides, you could even stop for a time of prayer after each half dozen or so. When prayer requests are presented, it is best to keep them short. Long detailed accounts for prayer not only kill the spirit of the meeting, but they also often leave very little time for prayer. Items for prayer and praise could be written in advance and given out to people as they arrive, or they could be written on a blackboard. One of the best helps is an overhead projector, especially as outline maps of various countries could also be shown.

Delegate individuals in advance to give a brief update on a particular country. This could include statistics (for example, the population of the region, its religion, etc. — all easily obtained from the book *Operation World*), something of the missionary work being done there, as well as any current news regarding different situations within that country. If the church has several missionaries, then play short tapes containing up-to-date information about their present circumstances. It may also be a good idea for pastors to encourage people to *adopt* a missionary family; to write to them regularly, and then to present briefly the needs of that family at the prayer meeting from time to time. It would be encouraging for both church members and the missionaries if mission fields could be visited now and again.

Urge different people to pray. Help them to feel relaxed in terms of grammar, theological content or length. Especially encourage those who don't pray very often or not at all—but don't embarrass anyone. There must be a balance between the Holy Spirit's spontaneous work and each person's helping to make the prayer meeting what it should be. Be patient and reject discouragement—people will not learn reality in prayer overnight. In order to encourage people to become more worldwide in their vision, it is good to make use of a world map and other helpful items (like the set of prayer cards).

Where and When

Where and how often should group prayer meetings be held? In addition to the weekly prayer meeting at the church, I strongly advise that the meeting be held periodically in homes. This opens doors of ministry through hospitality and avoids the pitfalls of isolating prayer from fellowship and basic spiritual growth. Around the world God is working in home meetings, and a church is foolish if it totally fails to make use of this opportunity in some way. How sad, on the other hand, to see many home groups having no real interest in praying for anything outside their own particular needs.

I believe there should be spontaneous early morning prayer meetings and days set aside for prayer, often far into the night. I believe this is one of the main factors in the victories we see around the world, both on our two ocean-going ships, and through our teams operating in more than twenty-five countries. During such extended times of prayer people must be made to feel free to leave when they want to. They must realize that they are not in a spiritual marathon. However, the more information they have about the world's needs, the more responsibility they will feel to pray for those needs to be met. And prayer takes time!

Remember we are in a spiritual warfare. Prayer is one of our main weapons and faith is closely linked with it. We must not expect it to be easy. Satan will counter-attack any efforts made towards effective prayer. We must refuse any form of discouragement and press forward whatever the cost. Half the world has still not heard or read the gospel and what we do in prayer, in God's sovereignty and mercy, will be a deciding factor as to whether or not they will. Let us ask God for new ideas and initiatives in order to be creative in the task that he has given us. And let us be disciplined in playing our personal part.[1]

13

The Highest Form of Christian Service

Oswald J. Smith

The highest form of Christian service is intercessory prayer. I state this without fear of contradiction. And what I am going to say now is applicable to every Christian in the world, for all may have a part. You may not be able to preach, but you can pray. It is your privilege to become an intercessor if you choose to, and thus accomplish the greatest work that God has committed to man.

Turn to Exodus 32:31-32, and notice here the almost unparalleled prayer of Moses as he intercedes on behalf of his people: "And Moses returned unto the Lord, and said. Oh, this people have sinned a great sin, and have made them gods of gold. Yet now, if Thou wilt forgive their sin –" And here occurs a pause indicated by a dash after the word "sin" as if Moses waited to hear God's answer before saying more, " – if Thou wilt forgive their sin," he prays. And in the pause that follows, his heart overwhelmed with grief, he listens for God's reply; but in vain he waits for an answer; there is no response. Then, with a burden that crushes him almost to death and a love that struggles up in his heart on behalf of his people, he continues his intercession: "And if not," he prays, "blot me, I pray Thee, out of Thy book which Thou hast written."

Oh, what a prayer! How marvelously this servant of God interceded for his people! What a burden rested heavy upon his heart! It is almost impossible for us to comprehend the bitter anguish of his soul as he pleaded. How deep was his love!

Did ever man pass through such an experience? And how feeble are our petitions in comparison with this great intercessor's! Moses was willing to be forever separated from God, to have his name blotted out of the Book of Life and be eternally lost, if only his people might be saved.

But Moses does not stand alone. There is one other who passed through the same experience, felt the same burden, endured the same agony and made same offer. That one was Paul, the mighty apostle to the Gentiles. "I say the truth in Christ," he exclaims, "I lie not, my conscience also bearing me witness in the Holy Ghost, that I have great heaviness and continual sorrow in my heart. For I could wish that I myself were accursed from Christ for my brethren, my kinsmen according to the flesh" (Rom. 9:1-3).

What a picture of the heart of Paul! We think of him as a man filled with joy, not only rejoicing himself, but bidding others to do the same. Yet here he declares that he has great heaviness and continual heart-sorrow, that he is under tremendous pressure, that he carries a burden every moment of the day and night. And, oh, what a burden! How it crushes him! So great is it that he declares himself willing to be accursed, eternally separated from Christ, for the sake of his kinsmen according to the flesh. In other words, Paul feels exactly the same as Moses felt. So wonderful is his love for his own people Israel, that, after counting the cost, he is willing to lose all in order that they might gain all. And the only relief he can find is in prayer, mighty, unceasing intercession for his brethren the Jews.

And now with such examples of intercession born out of a broken, burdened heart, how lamentably weak and unreal are our prayers! Would to God we too might be thus burdened for others, that we might have power with God in the ministry of intercession.

Now I want to mention some things which it is necessary to remember if we are to engage in this, the highest form of Christian service.

Standing on Praying Ground

First of all, it means that we must be standing on praying ground. That is to say, we must be certain that everything is right between us and God. Unless this is the case it is useless to even attempt to pray. "If I regard iniquity in my heart," declares the inspired Word, "the Lord will not hear me" (Psa. 66:18). That means that God will not even listen to my prayer, let alone answer it. To be standing on praying ground is to have put away every sin, to turn from anything that grieves the Holy Spirit, and to separate myself from all that is displeasing to God. And so as we think of this, the highest form of Christian service, and resolve to become intercessors, let us make sure first of all that we are standing on praying ground and that there is nothing between us and God.

The Burden for Others

In the second place, intercessory prayer means that we have prayed beyond ourselves, our needs and problems, and that we are in a place and position spiritually to enter into this blessed ministry with Jesus Christ, taking upon us the burden for others in a real soul-travail, and allowing the Holy Spirit to pray through us in the will of God.

Most of the prayers recorded in the Bible are for others. Moses and Paul, as we have already seen, thought only of Israel. Our Lord himself seldom prayed for his own needs. His burden was always for the multitudes that thronged him on every side. Intercessory prayer is prayer for others.

That means that we put ourselves alongside of the Lord Jesus Christ, seek to know the burden of his heart, find out the plan, the program that he wants carried out, and then pray with that in mind. So often we do not think of this. The whole burden of our prayer is centered upon ourselves. It is our needs, our desires, that are uppermost in our prayers. We must get past this. We must pray until we have dealt with everything that concerns ourselves and then launch out in intercession on behalf of others. What does God want done? What is his plan for this work or that? How best can we serve the interests of the Lord Jesus Christ and glorify him? These are the questions that must be asked. Let us therefore wait before him until he reveals the burden of his heart, and then, putting ourselves alongside Jesus Christ, let us intercede and bring his program to pass.

That means that we must take into account the enablement of the Holy Spirit, for he alone knows the mind of God. The life yielded to Him will be directed, guided and illuminated, so that the petitions offered will not miss the mark. He will lead us to pray along the line of God's plan and God's purpose if we will but trust him and place ourselves entirely at His disposal. Oh, the joy of praying with Jesus Christ! That is a different thing from praying for ourselves.

The Hardest Kind of Work

Now I want to go on and say that intercessory prayer is without doubt not only the highest form of Christian service, but also the hardest kind of work. To the person who is not an intercessor such a statement seems absurd. Prayer to most people is looked upon as an easy occupation. Difficulties are unknown. But that is because they know nothing at all of the ministry of intercession. Their prayers, for the most part, are centered upon themselves, their loved ones and their own personal interests, with an occasional petition for the perishing heathen. They spend, perchance, five to fifteen minutes in the morning and the same again at night. To set aside a special hour during the day, or to wait before God for half a night never enters their mind. Their prayer life is spasmodic. It is considered a side issue and is readily neglected if other things demand attention. Such a person is in no way affecting the kingdom of Satan. Hence prayer, so-called, is easy.

But the Christian who enters upon the ministry of intercession will pass through a very different experience. Satan will do everything in his power to hinder and obstruct. There will be a conscious realization of his presence and opposition.

Then, too, discouragement will cross our pathway. Again and again we will feel like giving up. No wonder the Lord gave the parable of the friend at midnight. Importunity is one of the greatest requisites. We pray on for a certain time and then because the answer does not come we grow discouraged and give up. Thus Satan uses his most successful weapon against us and breaks down our determination to become intercessors.

Then, when all else has failed, he will burden us with work. Satan would rather have us work than pray any time. Full well he knows that prayerless work will be powerless and fruitless. Hence if he can only keep us busy so that we do not have time to pray he will have accomplished his purpose.

Away with work that hinders prayer,
'Twere best to lay it down;
For prayerless work, however good,
Will fail to win the crown.

Oh, my brother, let me beg of you to take stock of your life and to make a thorough investigation and see if everything you are doing is really essential. Perhaps you are crowding out prayer by allowing Christian activities to take its place. I plead with you, before it is forever too late, to adjust your ministry, leave out the nonessentials and do not allow yourself to become overloaded, but see to it that you have time to get alone with God, and you will accomplish more in one month than you otherwise could in a year.

"Epaphras, who is one of you, a servant of Christ, saluteth you, always laboring fervently for you in prayers" (Col. 4:12). Why such fervency? Why so much labor? Most of us would simply make our request before God, believe that he had answered, and think no more about it. But not so with Epaphras. To him it was hard work. He was a real intercessor. And so Paul describes his prayer life on behalf of others not only as labor but "fervent labor," or, as it is in the margin, "striving." Do we know anything about that kind of ministry?

"And being in an agony he prayed more earnestly: and his sweat was as it were great drops of blood falling down to the ground" (Luke 22:44). Thus prayed the Son of God. Even to him prayer was the most difficult work that he had to do. Oh yes, it was a joy, for communion with God always brings joy and blessing; but then there is the enemy to meet when prayer becomes a battle. I wonder how much we know about this kind of prayer?

The inspired Word says that he was in agony, that after he had prayed for a time he began to pray more earnestly, and that the work was so hard, the agony so great, the burden so heavy, the pressure so terrible, that the very sweat became blood as it oozed out through the pores of his skin. What intensity! How terrific the struggle! And how far we fall short in our intercessory prayer life! How little we know of the burden that rested on the Son of God.

"Likewise the Spirit also helpeth our infirmities: for we know not what we should pray for as we ought: but the Spirit himself maketh intercession for us with groanings which cannot be uttered" (Rom. 8:26). Here we have a picture of the prayer life of the Holy Spirit. Even he prays as Jesus prayed. Note the language used in regard to his intercession: it was with "groanings." And in order to give some idea of the intensity and suffering it is said that the groans of the Spirit are inexpressible. No language is capable of conveying an adequate conception of the fervency of the Spirit's intercessions. They are with groanings which cannot be uttered.

Thy Most Effective Weapon

Intercessory prayer is the Christian's most effective weapon. Nothing can withstand its power. It will do things when all else has failed. And the marvel is that we turn to other agencies in order to accomplish what only prayer can bring to pass. God has placed this mighty weapon in our hands and he expects us to use it. How disappointed he must be when we lay it aside and substitute natural means for supernatural work.

When D. L. Moody (1837-1899) first visited Edinburgh, Scotland, it was literally true that within a few days the entire city was stirred to its depths. Not only so, but the whole of Scotland was more or less aroused. It was not long until the trains were bringing people into the city to attend the meetings from every part of the country, so tremendous was the interest.

What had happened? Why, God in answer to volumes of intercessory prayer that for months past had been ascending daily, had suddenly put a great concern upon the people. Thousands became anxious about their spiritual condition, and multitudes were swept into the Kingdom. It was one of the greatest, if not the greatest, outpourings of the Spirit that Scotland has ever seen or known. And now what is the result? Was it a true outcome ?

I was over in the Old Country a few months ago, and this is what I discovered. The great outstanding leaders in evangelical and evangelistic work all over the British Isles, the men and women who have accomplished the biggest things for God's Kingdom, in the large majority of cases, were converted under the ministry of D. L. Moody. Scotland has never forgotten that remarkable visitation. The secret, as everyone will admit, was first and foremost, intercessory prayer.

"The effectual fervent prayer of a righteous man availeth much" (James 5:16). Such is God's estimate of intercessory prayer. The illustration that follows is taken from the ministry of Elijah. How marvelously he made use of the God-appointed method! I think of Elijah as walking around with the key of Heaven in his pocket. Taking it out, he places it in the lock of the clouds, turns it, and lo, the heavens are shut and closed, so that no rain can possibly fall. Three and a half years later he takes the key again from his pocket, puts it in the same lock, turns it, and lo, the rain falls in torrents. Thus he wielded the mighty weapon of intercession and brought things to pass.

"Peter therefore was kept in prison: but prayer was made without ceasing of the church unto God for him" (Acts 12:5). Yes, Peter was kept in prison, that was man's power. Then follow two words that bring us immediately into a higher realm where mightier forces are at work — "But prayer." Thank God, the Early Church knew the power of intercessory prayer. Peter was released. God had sent His angel in answer to the cry of the Church.

Why have we turned away from it? How is it that the Church of today has such little confidence in the efficacy of intercession? What a loss is ours! Oh, that God might talk loudly to us and call us back to the days of the Early Church, until once again we are brought to realize the effectiveness of this mighty weapon, so that we, too, may bring things to pass and do a supernatural work through intercessory prayer.

The High-water Mark

Intercessory prayer is the high-water mark of spiritual experience. There are many who boast of wonderful supernatural manifestations who are not intercessors. It is possible to have some of the gifts of the Spirit, and yet not to be an intercessor. To fail here is to fail everywhere, but to thus enter into fellowship with Christ is the greatest of all blessings.

You can never get higher than the throne-life. When Jesus Christ returned to the right hand of his Father it was to engage in the great ministry of intercession on behalf of his Church. For nineteen hundred years now he has been occupied in this way. In his estimation at least it is the most important work that he has to do. The throne-life is the high-water mark. To engage in this same ministry is to do down here what

Christ is doing up there. The Bible says, "He ever liveth to make intercession for them" (Heb. 7:25).

My friend, you may be seeking some special gift. You may be looking for some unusual manifestation. It may be that some great emotional experience is your delight, and possibly you look down upon others who have not as yet received what you have received and consider that you are far above them in Christian experience. Let me assure you that such is not the case. The highest form of Christian service is intercessory prayer. The high-water mark of spiritual experience is an intercessory life. Unless you have attained to this you fall far short. I care not how emphatically you may boast of your spiritual experiences and of the special gifts that you have received, your ministry is void of power, your gifts valueless, if you know not how to intercede on behalf of others. The throne-life is what really counts with God.

Forgive me if I seem to speak strongly on this point. But we are living in a day when Satan has substituted everything else in the world for spirituality in the place of intercessory prayer. We need to be warned and placed on our guard lest we be deceived by his devices and miss after all the high-water mark of spiritual experience.

God's Mighty Instrument

Intercessory prayer is God's mighty instrument for the salvation of souls. I give here as an example the remarkable conversion of J. Hudson Taylor (1832-1905) as related in his own words. It shows how his mother's prayers prevailed on his behalf. With gifts and talents she was not especially endowed, but she knew God, and she knew the ministry that is carried on behind the closed door. The incident reads as follows:

> Little did I know at the time what was going on in the heart of my dear mother, seventy or eighty miles away. She rose from the dinner table that afternoon with an intense yearning for the conversion of her boy, and feeling that—absent from home, and having more leisure than she could otherwise secure—a special opportunity was afforded her of pleading with God on my behalf, she went to her room and turned the key in the door, resolved not to leave that spot until her prayers were answered. Hour after hour that dear mother pled for me, until at length she could pray no longer, but was constrained to

praise God for that which His Spirit taught her had already been accomplished — the conversion of her only son.

When our dear mother came home a fortnight later, I was the first to meet her at the door, and to tell her I had such glad news to give. I can almost feel that dear mother's arms around my neck, as she pressed me to her bosom, and said, "I know, my boy; I have been rejoicing for a fortnight in the glad tidings you have to tell me."

Oh, my friends, may God stir our hearts! How great is our responsibility! How wonderful are our resources! Souls are perishing on every side. Many of our relatives and loved ones are still outside the fold. We have talked to them and urged them to accept Christ, but all in vain. Year after year has gone by and they are not yet saved. Oh, that we might take upon us the burden of their souls and give God no rest until he answers and they are converted. If we truly realize the mighty instrument that God has placed in our hands we will surely wield it until results are obtained. All else may fail, but intercessory prayer is bound to avail. God cannot deny himself.

God's All-Powerful Agency

Intercessory prayer is God's all powerful agency for the outpouring of the Spirit. No revival has ever yet been given apart from this ministry. Someone has prayed. Go, if you will, to the records of the great awakenings for years past and you will find that the secret, the source, has been prayer. God has burdened a little group here and there, sometimes only two or three in number, but these have so given themselves to intercessory prayer that the result has been a mighty outpouring of the Holy Spirit.

The mystery of the great awakening under D. L. Moody in the church where he preached one Sunday night in England, when hundreds were swept into the Kingdom, for some time remained unsolved, but at last the secret came to light. Two sisters, we were told, lived together. One was an invalid. Some years before she had picked up a newspaper and read an account of the work of the great American evangelist, D. L. Moody. A burden settled down upon her. From that day she began to pray that God would send Moody to England and that he might preach in her church. At last after praying daily her request was granted. Her sister came home one morning and told her that a man by the name of Moody had preached.

Under a great burden the invalid shut herself in and refused to be seen. All that afternoon she pled with God, with the result that showers of blessing fell upon the congregation and hundreds were saved at the close of the evening service. That was the beginning of Moody's great work in the British Isles. God had signally set to His seal and it all came about as the result of an invalid's intercession.

When I was holding a city-wide campaign in Ballymena, where I faced the largest crowds that had ever gathered, I went to the little old school house where the four young men had wrestled with God in prayer, prayer that resulted in the great Irish Revival of 1859 — travailing, prevailing prayer.

Let me quote from the lectures of Charles G. Finney (1792-1875), the man who prayed down revivals. This incident proves again that God's all powerful agency in true revival work is intercessory prayer. It reads as follows:

A pious man in the western part of this state [New York] was suffering from consumption. He was a poor man, and was ill for years. An unconverted merchant in the place, who had a kind heart, used to send him now and then some things for his comfort, or for his family. He felt grateful for the kindness, but could make no return, as he wanted to do. At length he determined that the best return he could make would be to pray for the man's salvation. So he began to pray, and his soul kindled, and he got hold of God. No revival was taking place there, but, by and by, to the astonishment of everybody, this merchant came right out on the Lord's side. The fire kindled all over the place, a powerful revival followed, and multitudes were converted.

This poor man lingered, in this condition of weakness, for several years. After his death, I visited the place, and his widow put into my hands his diary. Among other entries was this: "I am acquainted with about thirty ministers and churches." He then went on to set apart certain hours in the day and week to pray for each of these ministers and churches, and also certain seasons for praying for different missionary stations. Then followed, under different dates, such facts as these: "Today I have been enabled to offer what I call the prayer of faith for the outpouring of the Spirit on ---------- Church, and I trust in God there will soon be a revival there." Under another date he had written: "I have today been able to offer what I call the prayer of faith for ---------- Church and trust there will soon be a revival there." Thus he had gone over a great number of churches, recording the fact that he had prayed for them in faith that a revival might soon prevail among them, and it did. She told me that he was so exercised in prayer during his sickness, that she often feared he would pray himself to death. The revival was exceedingly great and powerful in all the region, and the fact that it was about to prevail had not been hidden from this servant of the Lord. According to his Word, "the secret of the Lord is with them that fear him" (Psa. 25: 14). Thus this man, too feeble in body to go out of his house, was yet more useful to the world and the Church of God than all the heartless professors in the country. Standing between God and the desolations of Zion, and pouring out his heart in believing prayer, "as a prince he had power with God and with men, and prevailed" (Gen. 32:28).

There are two kinds of means requisite to promote a revival: the one to influence men, the other to influence God. Prayer is an essential link in the chain of causes that lead to a revival, as much so as truth is. Some have zealously used truth to convert men, and laid very little stress on prayer. They have preached, and talked, and distributed tracts with great zeal, and then wondered that they had so little success. And the reason was that they forgot to use the other branch of the means, effectual prayer. They overlooked the fact that truth, by itself, will never produce the effect, without the Spirit of God, and that the Spirit is given in answer to prayer.

Prayer and the Word

There is one passage in the Bible that has been more or less of a motto to me for years past. It is the statement found in Acts 6:4, and reads as follows: "We will give ourselves continually to prayer and to the ministry of the Word." What an ideal vocation! Everything else was considered secondary. The greatest thing that the apostles could possibly do for the Kingdom of God was to give themselves first to prayer, then to the ministry of the Word. And you will notice that prayer precedes preaching.

Oh, my brethren, let me entreat you to lay greater emphasis on this part of your work. To minister the Word apart from prayer is impossible. The two are inseparably connected. He who would preach powerfully must pray effectively. To prevail with God is to prevail with man. Therefore let us give ourselves as never before in these closing days of the age to intercessory prayer, the highest form of Christian service.

14

We Thank Thee, Lord, for Using Us

Horatius Bonar

We thank Thee, Lord, for using us
For Thee to work and speak;
However trembling is the hand,
The voice however weak.

We bless Thee for each seed of truth
That we through Thee have sowed
Upon this waste and barren earth —
The living seed of God.

We thank Thee, gracious God, for all
Of witness there hath been
From us, in any path of life,
Though silent and unseen.

For solace ministered perchance
In days of grief and pain;
For peace to troubled, weary souls,
Not spoken all in vain.

Lord, keep us still the same as in

Remembered days of old;
O keep us fervent still in love,
Mid many waxing cold.

Help us, O Christ, to grasp each truth
With hand as firm and true,
As when we clasped it first to heart,
A treasure fresh and new:

Thy name to name, Thyself to own
With voice unfaltering,
And face as bold and unashamed
As in our Christian spring.

Of honour higher, truer far
Than earthly fame could bring,
Thus to be used, in work like this,
So long, by such a King.[1]

15

On Maintaining a Life of Prayer

François Fénelon

Two main points of attention are necessary to maintain a constant spirit of prayer that unites us with God. We must continually seek to cherish it, and we must avoid everything that tends to make us lose it.

In order to cherish it, we should follow a regular course of reading; we must have appointed times of secret prayer and frequently recall our minds consciously to God during the day. We should make use of quiet days or retreats when we feel the need of them or when they are advised by those more experienced than we whose counsel we seek, and when our other responsibilities allow for them.

We should be very afraid of all things that have a tendency to make us lose this state of prayer and be very careful to avoid them. Thus we should avoid those worldly activities and associates which turn our minds in the wrong direction, and those pleasures which excite the passions. We should avoid everything calculated to awaken the love of the world and those old inclinations that have caused us so much trouble.

There are many details that might apply in dealing with cherishing the spirit of prayer and avoiding that which works against it. Because each individual case has features peculiar to itself, only general directions can be given here.

We should choose books which instruct us in our duty and in our faults; which, while they point to the greatness of God, teach us what our duty is to him and how very far we are from perfecting it. We should not seek those emotional publications which melt and sentimentalize the heart. The tree must bear fruit. We can only judge the life of the root by the fruit it bears.[1]

The first effect of a sincere love is an earnest desire to know all that we ought to do to gratify the one we love. Any other desire is an indication that we love ourselves under a pretense of loving God. It shows that we are seeking an empty and deceitful consolation in him, that we want to use God for our pleasure, instead of sacrificing that pleasure for his glory. God forbid that his children should love him so! Cost what it may, if we want truly to love him, we must know what he requires of us and try to do it without reservation.

Periods of secret prayer must be determined by the time available, the disposition, the condition, and the inward leading of each individual.

A necessary foundation to prayer is meditating and thinking on the great truths which God has revealed. We should be familiar with all the mysteries of Jesus Christ and the truths of his gospel. Our souls should be colored by them and penetrated by them as wool is by dye. These truths should become so familiar to us that we acquire the habit of forming no judgment except in their light, that they may be our only guide in what we do, as the rays of the sun are our only light in what we see.

It is when these truths are inwardly incorporated in us that our praying begins to be real and fruitful. Up to that point prayer was but a shadow. We thought we had penetrated to the inmost depths of the gospel, when in truth we had barely set foot upon its border. All our most tender and ardent feelings, our firmest resolutions, our clearest and most distant visions were, in reality, but the rough and shapeless mass from which God would hew his likeness in us.

When his celestial rays begin to shine within us, then we see in the true light. Then we instantaneously assent to every truth in the same way we admit, without any process of reasoning, the splendor of the sun the moment we behold its rising beams. Our union with God must be the result of our faithfulness in doing and enduring all that he wills for us.

Our meditations should become deeper and more inward every day. I say deeper, because by frequent and humble meditation upon

God's truth, we penetrate further and further in search of new treasures; and more inward, because as we seek more and more to enter into these truths, they penetrate into the very substance of our souls. Then it will be that a simple word will go further than a whole sermon.

Our meditation should not be subtle or composed of long reasonings. Simple and natural reflections from the subject of our thoughts is all that is required. We need take but a few truths, meditate upon these without hurry, without effort, and without seeking for far-fetched reflections. Every truth should be considered with reference to its practical bearing in our lives. To receive it without using all means to put it faithfully into practice at whatever cost is to "hold the truth in unrighteousness."[2] It is a resistance to the truth that has been impressed upon us and, of course, is resistance to the Holy Spirit. This is the most terrible of all unfaithfulness.

As to a method of praying, each one must be guided by his or her own experience. If some find themselves aided in using a strict method, they need not depart from it. Those who cannot so confine themselves may make use of their own mode without judging that which has proved helpful to so many others. A method is intended to assist.

Growth in prayer is indicated by a growth in simplicity and steadiness in our attitude. Our conversation with God resembles that with a friend. At first there are a thousand things to be told, and just as many to be asked. After a time, however, these diminish, while the pleasure of being together does not. Everything has been said, but the satisfaction of seeing each other, of feeling that one is near the other, can be felt without conversation. The silence is eloquent and mutually understood. Each feels that the other is in perfect harmony with him, and that their two hearts are continuously being poured into each other, becoming one.

It is the same way in prayer. Our communion with God becomes a simple and familiar union, far beyond the need of words. But let it be remembered that God must initiate this kind of prayer within us. Nothing would be more rash nor more dangerous than to dare to attempt it of ourselves. We must allow ourselves to be led step by step, by someone conversant with the ways of God and who may lay the immovable foundations of correct teaching and of the complete death of self in everything.

Our practice of prayer in seclusion or private retirement must be regulated by our leisure and our other needs. We must attend to duty before we seek enjoyment in spiritual exercises. The man who has public duties and spends the time meditating that he should be giving to his duties, would miss God while he sought to be united to him. The true union with God is to do his will without ceasing in every duty of life, in spite of all natural disinclination, and however disagreeable or mortifying it may be to our self-will.

We must, however, reserve the necessary time that we may seek God alone in prayer. Those who have positions of importance to fill usually have so many indispensable duties to perform, that without the greatest care in the management of their time, there will be none left to be alone with God. If they have ever so little inclination for foolish amusement, the hours that belong to God and their neighbor disappear altogether.

We must be firm in observing our rules. This strictness seems excessive, but without it everything falls into confusion. We will become dissipated, relaxed, and spiritually weak. We will be unconsciously drawn away from God, surrendering ourselves to all our pleasures, and only begin to see that we have wandered when it is almost hopeless to think of trying to return.

Prayer, prayer! this is our only safety. "Praise be to God who has not rejected my prayer, or withheld his love from me."[3] To be faithful in prayer it is indispensable that we arrange all the activities of the day with a regularity that nothing can disturb.[4]

16

Praying in the Spirit

Samuel Chadwick

Early in the year 1882 there came to me an experience that lifted my life to a new plane of understanding and of power. I received the gift of the Holy Spirit. I was led in ways I did not know, for I had hardly so much as heard that such an experience was possible. The demands of an impossible task awakened me to a sense of need. I had neither power nor might in either service or prayer. I began to pray for power for service, and God led me to the answer by way of equipment for prayer.

It was a great surprise to me, for I thought I knew how to pray, and had prayed much over the work to which he had sent me. When I began to seek power, my ears were opened before my eyes began to see. I heard testimonies to which I had been deaf. Others had been driven to God baffled by lack of power, but they always associated the gift of power with an experience of holiness about which I was not keen.

It was power I wanted. I wanted power that I might succeed, and my chief concern for power was the success it would bring. I wanted success that would fill my church, save the people, and bring down the strong fortifications of Satan with a crash. I was young, and I was in a hurry. Twelve of us began to pray in band, and the answer came by

A way no more expected,
Than when His sheep
Passed through the deep,

By crystal walls protected.

He led us to Pentecost. The key to all my life is in that experience. It awakened my mind as well as cleansed my heart. It gave me a new joy and a new power, a new love and a new compassion. It gave me a new Bible and a new message. Above all else, it gave me a new understanding and a new intimacy in the communion and ministry of prayer; it taught me to pray in the Spirit.

The Cooperation of the Spirit

The work of the Holy Spirit is always in cooperation. He never works alone. He depends upon human cooperation for the mediation of his mind, the manifestation of truth, and the effectual working of his will. He indwells the body of Christ, as Christ dwelt in the body prepared for him by the Holy Spirit. Revelation came from the Spirit of Truth as men of God were inspired by him. The Word is his, but the writing is with the hands of men. This twofold action runs through the whole of redemption by Christ Jesus.

Our Lord was born of a woman, but was conceived by the Holy Spirit of God. He grew in stature and in knowledge in the house of Joseph, instructed and guided by the Holy Spirit. His teaching and ministry were in the power of the same Spirit. He offered himself without blemish unto God through the Eternal Spirit, and it was the Spirit that raised up Christ from the dead.

There is the same cooperation in all the experience of salvation. There is always a human and a divine factor. There is a twofold witness, a twofold leading, a twofold work, and a twofold intercession. We pray in the Spirit, and the Spirit maketh intercession for us.

The Fellowship of The Spirit in Prayer

The Holy Spirit does nothing of himself, neither does he do anything for himself. His mission is to glorify Christ, and all he does is based upon the finished work of Christ. He could not be given until Jesus was glorified, and in experience there can be no Pentecost until there is a coronation. The Spirit is the coronation gift of Jesus, whom the Father has made to be both Lord and Christ. The fellowship of the Spirit in prayer is made possible by an experience in Christ.

The sequence is set forth in the eighth chapter of Romans (verses 9-27). Those who pray in the Spirit must be in the Spirit, and if the Spirit of God is to make intercession for us, he must dwell in us. If we live after the flesh, we die; if we are led of the Spirit, and walk not after the flesh, but after the Spirit, then the Spirit dwells in us, lives through us, and works by us. Then comes to pass that which is written:

And, in like manner the Spirit also helpeth our infirmity: for we know not how to pray as we ought; but the Spirit himself [that dwelleth in us] maketh intercession for us with groanings which cannot be uttered; and he that searcheth the hearts knoweth what is the mind of the Spirit, because he maketh intercession for the saints according to the will of God.

The Holy Spirit searches the deep things of God. He takes of the things of Christ and reveals them unto us. God knows the mind of the Spirit; we pray in the Spirit, instructed and inspired by him, and he makes intercession for us in word less intercession. That is the New Testament explanation of prayer that prevails. Though I did not know it until years after, that is what happened to me when God gave me a new understanding, a new joy, and a new power in prayer. A new Personality entered a new temple, and set up a new altar. As I live, yet not I; so I pray, yet not I; I pray in the Spirit, and the Spirit himself also makes intercession. The Spirit in my spirit prays.

The Spirit Helping Our Infirmities

He instructs and inspires all true prayer. There is no truer word than that "we know not what we should pray for as we ought." There is no realm in which we so soon come to the end of what we know as in that of prayer. Our petitions urge wants that are immediate, obvious, and urgent. We cannot see deep enough or far enough to know what is real need.

Most people would like good health, home comfort, congenial conditions, happy friendships, a little more money, and better success; but who can tell if these would be for their ultimate good? God sees deeper and farther, and he may will otherwise. How often have people who have pleaded with breaking hearts that a life might be spared lived to thank God that the Lord took when he did? He knew what was coming, and took them from the evil to come. The Holy Spirit knows the mind of Christ and the will of God, and he teaches us how to pray and what to pray for. If any man lack wisdom, let him ask of God, and he will give him more than wisdom, he will give him the Spirit of wisdom to instruct, strengthen, and guide.

The Holy Spirit creates the conditions of prayer. We may ask amiss, not only in what we ask, but also in the reason for asking. He sanctifies desire and directs it into the will of God, so that we desire what God wills to give. That is how it comes to pass that if we delight ourselves in the Lord, we can be sure that he will give us the desires of our heart. We want what he wills.

The Spirit brings to expression the unutterable things of the soul. His groanings are before our praying, and our prayers are born of His travail. In him is the supply of life and desire, wisdom and faith, intercession and power. He quickens desire, purifies motive, inspires confidence, and assures faith.

The Prayer of the Spirit

This is the inner meaning of prayer. It is more than asking, it is communion, fellowship, cooperation, identification with God the Father and the Son by the Holy Spirit. Prayer is more than words, for it is mightiest when wordless. It is more than asking, for it reaches its highest glory when it adores and asks nothing. When a child entered his father's study and walked up to him at his desk, the father turned and asked, "What did you want, Sonny?" The little chap answered, "Nothing, daddy, I just came to be with you."

This mystery of the Spirit is the key to other mysteries. The secret of the Lord is made manifest to those who pray in the fellowship of the Spirit. There are stages of prayer. In one stage we pray and ask him to help. There is a more wonderful way in which he prays and we assent, and his praying is ours. He makes intercession within the temple of our hearts, and our Lord ever lives to make intercession for us at the right hand of the Father. The Spirit within our spirits prays, working in us to will and to do the will and good pleasure of our Father which is in Heaven. He is God the Spirit representing God the Father, and God the Son, and the three are one God. He is the power that works in us. He it is that unifies hearts in prayer and makes them an irresistible unity in intercession. The assurance of answered prayer comes from him, and he it is that makes prayer the mightiest force in the universe of God. The secret of it all is in him. The power of it all is by him. The joy of it all is with him. The biggest thing God ever did for me was to teach me to pray in the Spirit.

We are never really men of prayer in the best sense, until we are filled with the Holy Ghost. Therefore, Lord, teach us to pray in the Spirit![1]

17

She Prayed All Night

R. A. Torrey

I shall never forget a scene I witnessed many years ago in Boston. It was at the International Christian Workers' Convention which was held in the old Tremont Temple, seating thirty-five hundred people. It was my privilege to preside at the Convention. On a Saturday morning at eleven o'clock the Tremont Temple was packed to its utmost capacity, every inch of standing room where men and women were allowed to stand was taken, and multitudes outside still clamoring for admission.

The audience was as fine in its quality as it was large in its numbers. As I looked back of me on the platform, it seemed as if every leading minister and clergyman not only of Boston but also of New England was on that platform. As I looked down in front of me I saw seated there the leaders in not only the church life but in the social and commercial and political life of Boston and the surrounding country. I rose to announce the next speaker on the program; and my heart sank, for the next speaker was a woman. In those days I had a prejudice against any women speaking in public under any circumstances. But this particular woman was a professing Christian, and a Presbyterian.

She had been what we call a "worldly Christian," a dancing, card-playing, theater-going, low-necked dressed Christian. She had had, however, an experience of which I had not heard. One night, sitting in their beautiful home in New York City, for she was a woman of wealth, she turned to her husband as he sat reading the evening paper and said:

"Husband, I hear they are doing a good work down at Jerry McAuley's Mission, let us go down and help them." He laid aside his paper and said: "Well, let us go." They put on their coats and started for Jerry McAuley's Mission.

When they got there they found the Mission Hall full and took seats back by the door. As they sat there and listened to one after another of those rescued men, they were filled with new interest, a new world seemed opening to them; and yet at last the woman turned to her husband and whispered: "I guess they will have to help us instead of our helping them. They've got something we haven't."

And when the invitation was given out, this finely-dressed, cultured gentleman and his wife went forward and knelt down at the altar in the sawdust along with drunken men and other outcasts of the waterfront, and they experienced real salvation.

But of this I knew nothing. I only knew the type of woman she had been, and when I saw her name on the program my heart sank and I thought, "What a waste of a magnificent opportunity. Here is this wonderful audience and only this woman to speak to them." But I had no authority to change the program; my business was simply to announce it. And summoning all the courtesy I could command under the circumstances, I introduced this lady, and then sank into the chairman's seat and buried my face in my hands and began to pray to God to save us from disaster.

Some years afterwards I was in the city of Atlanta, and one of the leading Christian workers of that city, who had been at the Boston Convention, came to me and said: "I shall never forget how you introduced Mrs. Whittemore at the Boston Convention, and then dropped into your chair and covered your face with hands as if you had done something you were ashamed of."

Well, I had. But as I said, I began to pray. In a little while I took my face out of my hands and began to watch as well as pray. Every one of those thirty-five hundred pairs of eyes was riveted on that little woman as she stood there and spoke.

Soon I saw tears come into eyes that were unaccustomed to weeping, and I saw men and women taking out their handkerchiefs and at first trying to pretend they were not weeping, and then, throwing all disguise to the winds, I saw them bow their heads on the backs of the seats in front of them and sob as if their hearts would break. And before that wonderful address was over that whole audience was swept by the power of that woman's words, as the trees of our Western forests are sometimes swept by the cyclone.

This was Saturday morning. The following Monday morning Dr. Broadbeck, at that time pastor of the leading Methodist Church in Boston, came to me and said with a choking voice, "Brother Torrey, I could not open my mouth to speak to my own people in my church yesterday morning without bursting into tears as I thought of that wonderful scene we witnessed here on Saturday morning."

When that wonderful address was over, some of us went to this woman and said to her: "God has wonderfully used you this morning."

"Oh," she replied, "would you like to know the secret of it? Last night as I thought of the great throng that would fill the Tremont Temple this morning, and of my own inexperience in public address, I spent the whole night on my face before God in prayer."

Oh, men and women, if we would spend more nights before God on our faces in prayer, there would be more days of power when we faced our congregations![1]

18

Distractions in Prayer

Frederick William Faber

Ah dearest Lord! I cannot pray,
My fancy is not free;
Unmannerly distractions come,
And force my thoughts from Thee.

The world that looks so dull all day
Glows bright on me at prayer,
And plans that ask no thought but then
Wake up and meet me there.

All nature one full fountain seems
Of dreamy sight and sound,
Which, when I kneel, breaks up its deeps,
And makes a deluge round.

Old voices murmur in my ear,
New hopes start to life,
And past and future gaily blend
In one bewitching strife.

My very flesh has restless fits;

My changeful limbs conspire
With all these phantoms of the mind
My inner self to tire.

I cannot pray; yet, Lord! Thou knowest
The pain it is to me
To have my vainly struggling thoughts
Thus torn away from Thee.

Sweet Jesus! teach me how to prize
These tedious hours when I,
Foolish and mute before Thy Face,
In helpless worship lie.

Prayer was not meant for luxury,
Or selfish pastime sweet;
It is the prostrate creature's place
At his Creator's Feet.

Had I, dear Lord, no pleasure found
But in the thought of Thee,
Prayer would have come unsought, and been
A truer liberty.

Yet Thou art oft most present, Lord!
In weak distracted prayer:
A sinner out of heart with self
Most often finds Thee there.

For prayer that humbles sets the soul
From all illusions free,
And teaches it how utterly,
Dear Lord, it hangs on Thee.

The heart, that on self-sacrifice

Is covetously bent,
Will bless Thy chastening hand that makes
Its prayer its punishment.

My Saviour! why should I complain
And why fear aught but sin?
Distractions are but outward things;
Thy peace dwells far within.

These surface-troubles come and go,
Like rufflings of the sea;
The deeper depth is out of reach
To all, my God, but Thee.[1]

19

Drawing Near
(Part 1)

Ralph I. Tilley

A recurring refrain rising from the hearts of all God-thirsty men and women since the dawn of creation is this: "Draw me nearer to you, O God!"

Such a cry has been implanted by the Father in the soul of every genuine convert from the moment of Spirit-birth. It may be articulated in a thousand different ways throughout one's pilgrimage here on earth, but whatever form the words take, they express one essential desire — "O God, I want to be near you! Draw me nearer, nearer!"

It was this desire that led innocent and undefiled Adam to stroll with Elohim in the Garden's coolness day by day; he delighted to be near his Creator. In blessed uninterrupted communion, the first man enjoyed unbroken fellowship before the tragic Fall. His joy was divine; the Garden was Heaven on earth. Why? Because God was near Adam and Adam was near God. The two walked together without the slightest foreign intrusion.

The Great Divide

With the Fall came both death and distance. Where life had reigned before, physical and spiritual death were to become commonplace. A severe fissure had occurred in man's relation to God. Suddenly, where there had been sweet and constant communion, there was now alienation and isolation. Man was cut off from his Maker. Instead of facing God, he runs from God. Instead of walking in open transparency with his Creator, he seeks to hide from him.

There is now rebellion against God, rationalization of his sin, malice toward his companion, and a dreadful fear of Elohim. "To complete all," says Adam Clarke (1760-1832), "the garden of pleasure is interdicted, and this man, who was made after the image of God, and who would be like him, [was] shamefully expelled from a place where pure spirits alone could dwell."[1] Life on earth was radically altered for Adam and Eve, and for all their progeny.

After the Fall, man began the futile journey of trying to reach God through his own ingenuity and will-power, and redeem himself through his self-effort. Fig leaves were the symbolic moral attempt to cover his own iniquity.

But God would have none of it. Man was incapable of initiating and engineering his own salvation. He had dug himself into a deep, dark pit by choosing his own way — turning inward instead of gazing upward and outward. God must take the initiative if man is to be saved from himself. Man had reached for what he wanted and got it — so he originally thought. That is what sin is, according to Dr. Dennis Kinlaw: "Sin is simply turning your eyes away from God and reaching for what you want."[2]

The Promised "Bridge"

The chasm created by the Fall must now be bridged in order for man to live near to God again. The "bridge" necessary to span this great divide would be designed and constructed by God himself — a bridge "foreknown before the foundation of the world" (1 Pet. 1:20).[3] Before man ever was driven from the Garden, the Lord God mercifully indicated such a bridge in pronouncing his curse on the serpent, as recorded in Genesis 3:15: "I will put enmity between you and the woman, and between your offspring and her offspring; he shall bruise your head, and you shall bruise his heel."

Matthew Henry's (1662-1714) comments on this passage are representative of evangelical theology: "A gracious promise is here made of Christ, as the deliverer of fallen man from the power of Satan. Though what was said was addressed to the serpent, yet it was said in the hearing of our first parents, who, doubtless, took the hints of grace here given them, and saw a door of hope opened to them, else the following sentence upon themselves would have overwhelmed them. Here was the dawning of the gospel day. No sooner was the wound given than the remedy was provided and revealed."[4]

Satan would be used by the Sovereign Lord to "bruise" Messiah's "heel" at Calvary; the same Sovereign Lord would "bruise" Satan's "head" by providing the atoning sacrifice for man's redemption through the voluntary death of his Son. Satan would be irretrievably defeated; man's salvation would be secured. Christ is Victor!

The Unfolding Prelude

Following the Fall, we read the unfolding prelude of God's promised salvation for mankind. From Genesis 3 to Matthew 2, God's purpose and plan for man's redemption deliberately, slowly, methodically, and persistently take shape. God selected one man (Abraham) through whom a new people (Israel) would be formed. Another man (Moses) was chosen through whom the Law would be given to Israel. Countless priests, prophets, and kings all played significant parts in God's unfolding prelude—a prelude that would culminate with God's own orchestrated Crescendo—the revelation of Messiah—God's Anointed One, his very own unique Son.

The "Interim" Answer

There was a time when if man drew too near to God it meant death. Before the Law was given to Moses on Mount Sinai, he was directed by God to approach him with specific conditions: "for on the third day the LORD will come down on Mount Sinai in the sight of all the people. And you shall set limits for the people all around, saying, 'Take care not to go up into the mountain or touch the edge of it. Whoever touches the mountain shall be put to death'" (Ex. 19:11-12). Because of man's pervasive sinfulness and Yahweh's inherent holiness, man was forbidden to even "touch" Mount Sinai.

Following a subsequent encounter with Yahweh, it was said of Moses: "Thus the LORD used to speak to Moses face to face, as a man speaks to his friend" (Ex. 33:11). At this time of God's unfolding salvation-plan, only Moses was permitted to come so close to God; only Moses enjoyed such a special relationship. Moses required no intermediary, yet even Moses' relationship with Yahweh was incomplete.

During the millennia leading up to the disclosure of God's ultimate and final remedy for man's salvation, God prescribed an "interim" answer for man's desire to draw near to his Creator-God. The answer was given to his specially selected people Israel through Moses on Sinai. The plan involved a local place of worship (tabernacle and later temple). At this Meeting Place, man would approach God by offering prescribed sacrifices to mediators, the priests. The priests in turn would present sinful man's sacrifices to a holy God. Man's sins were thereby expiated. God was pleased; man was forgiven.

However, the system was faulty. Only a select few people were permitted to approach God directly — to draw near to God. Levitical priests were prescribed by God to approach him twice daily and on special occasions, but they were forbidden to come any closer than the Altar of Burt Offering and the Holy Place. No common priest would dare enter the second sacred compartment — The Holy of Holies. Only Aaron, the Great High Priest (and his appointed successors) was allowed to enter this sacred place, and that only once each year when blood was sprinkled over the Mercy Seat for the peoples' unintentional sins. The Holy of Holies was God's Dwelling Place.

But there was never a time after which a worshiper had presented his sacrifice to a priest, or after a priest had offered prescribed sacrifices to Yahweh, or after the Great High Priest had annually brought the appointed blood into the Holy of Holies — there was never a time when that priest or worshiper left the Meeting Place feeling complete. The system was inadequate, deficient. Man could only come so near to Yahweh; Yahweh could only come so near to man. Man was accepted by God by following the prescribed ritual offered in faith, but his consciousness of God was unsatisfied and his conscience sorely imperfect.

The Perfect Remedy

God, however, was not found "asleep at the switch." The inadequacy of the old system was answered by the inauguration of a new system by a new Man. With the incarnation of his own unique Son, the loving Father revealed to Adam's lost posterity a name superior to those of angels, a hope surpassing all others, a covenant better than the former (which was based on better promises), an offering superseding any ever offered on Israel's altars, a high priest outranking every other.[5]

God's answer to man's dilemma — man's alienation, death, sin, lostness, and distance — was God in Christ. Redemption came through Christ; reconciliation was made through Christ; man is both declared and made righteous through Christ; adoption and sealing, communion and fellowship, forgiveness and sanctification, eternal life and abundant life — all these, and so much more — are found in Christ and Christ alone.

It is because of what God has accomplished and provided for us through his Son, and because of the Son's continuing, perpetual ministry, that all believers can now draw near to God. He is fully qualified to be the mediator between God and men. "He is," says the late evangelical scholar, F. F. Bruce (1900-1990), "the Prophet through whom God has spoken his final word to men; He is the Priest who has accomplished a perfect work for cleansing for His people's sins; He is the King who sits enthroned in the place of chief honor alongside the Majesty on high."[6]

The Book of Hebrews is the most comprehensive New Testament epistle addressing this subject of the believer's privilege of drawing near to God. This book provides its readers with the doctrinal basis for this privilege. I want to now note some select passages from this letter on this subject.

The Believer is Made Complete by Drawing Near to God

I intentionally chose the word "complete" in the above heading because our evangelical ears are so often shocked whenever we hear the word "perfect" with respect to anything having to do with God's work in us. And yet we dare not construe God's inspired words to mean anything less than what God intended — assuming the Spirit can help us to understand his words correctly (which I believe is a correct assumption for serious seekers of truth). Now for our first text: "For since the law was but a shadow of the good things to come instead of the true form of these realities, it can never, by the same sacrifices that are continually offered every year, make perfect those who draw near" (Heb. 10:1).

The Greek verb (*teleiosai*) in this passage is translated "make perfect" by four of today's major Bible versions (NASB, NRSV NIV, ESV). A good synonym for the word is "complete." While this is not the place to explore the meaning of all the occurrences of the word "perfect" in Scripture, a good working definition we can use for this particular context is, "lacking nothing essential for the whole."[7]

In Hebrews 10, the writer is contrasting the two covenants. He says the Old Covenant worshipers could never be perfected through their many sacrifices. And then he justifies his statement by asking a logical question: "Otherwise, would they not have ceased to be offered, since the worshipers, having once been cleansed, would no longer have any consciousness of sins?" (Heb. 10:2). The obvious answer to his question is, "Yes, if the Old Covenant worshipers had, indeed, experienced a perfect inner moral cleansing of sin, they consequently would not have been burdened with a continual consciousness of sin."

The writer takes his reasoning further: "But in these sacrifices there is a reminder of sins every year" (Heb. 10:3).

Two observations: First, because the worshiper's consciousness of sin was ongoing, his need to offer repeated sacrifices was necessary. Second, the writer has in view here the annual sacrifices offered on the Day of Atonement — Yom Kippur — ("every year"). This was the great day in Israel when her high priest followed a prescribed set of rituals for the nation's cleansing. It involved the offering and sprinkling of the blood of a bull and goats in the Holy of Holies, as well as the Azazel ceremony. Why was this day so significant? God gives us the reason: "For on this day shall atonement be made for you to cleanse you. You shall be clean before the LORD from all your sins" (Lev. 16:30).

But being "clean before the LORD" is not the same as being morally pure within. While the worshiper under the Old Covenant was justified by faith before God, he retained a consciousness of sin. God resolved this disparity through the sacrificial gift of his Son. The God who enacted the sacrificial system under the Old Covenant, ushered in a new system through the Lord Jesus Christ. Thus, the Spirit moved the writer of Hebrews to write these words within forty years following Christ's atoning death: "For it is impossible for the blood of bulls and goats to take away sins. Consequently, when Christ came into the world, he said, "Sacrifices and offerings you have not desired, but a body have you prepared for me" (Heb. 10:4, 5).

Contemplating this profound reality centuries later, Isaac Watts (1674-1748) wrote:

Not all the blood of beasts
On Jewish altars slain
Could give the guilty conscience peace
Or wash away the stain.

But Christ, the heav'nly Lamb,
Takes all our sins away;
A sacrifice of nobler name
And richer blood than they.[8]

The worshiper under the old system drew near — as far as he could. He sacrificed as instructed but he walked away from the Meeting Place incomplete, dissatisfied. He worshiped Yahweh, he loved Yahweh, he walked in fellowship with Yahweh. But guilt the consciousness of sins persisted.

It was only and finally through the once-for-all offering of the body of God's Son that perfection was made possible to the believer. What kind of perfection? In the context of Hebrews 10:1-7, it was the perfection of a cleansed consciousness of sin.

Thrilled with this truth, Charles Wesley (1707-1788) wrote:

With confidence I now draw nigh,
And, "Father, Abba, Father," cry.[9]

It is now our privilege to draw near to God. Why do we hesitate? Jesus has opened the way for us.

Let us draw near . . .

Drawing Near
(Part 2)

Ralph I. Tilley

I t was some time after my conversion experience that I discovered a passage of Scripture which informs believers of the essential keys in drawing near to God. It is located in an epistle that has become one of my favorites — *The Letter to the Hebrews*.

Having laid the groundwork in the previous chapters regarding the uniqueness, efficacy, all-sufficiency, and permanency of our heavenly High Priest, the Lord Jesus Christ, the writer proceeds to instruct his readers how they may now approach God, draw near to God as never before.

> Therefore, brothers, since we have confidence to enter the holy places by the blood of Jesus, by the new and living way that he opened for us through the curtain, that is, through his flesh, and since we have a great priest over the house of God, let us draw near with a true heart in full assurance of faith, with our hearts sprinkled clean from an evil conscience and our bodies washed with pure water (Heb. 12:19-22).[1]

The First Key

The first key necessary in drawing near to God is to possess a "true heart." In biblical terminology, the heart is the center of man's spiritual being; it is the veritable fountainhead from which all thought, imagination, affection, desire, and action originates. God says that when approaching him, the condition of one's heart is not a frivolous matter.

To have a true, or a sincere heart, is to have a heart free from hypocrisy. In other words, when we approach the Omniscient One, we must not pretend to be someone we're not. This is no time to put on airs.

To hear some of God's people pray one would think he was listening to a glorified saint—all the boasting and bragging about how good he or she is. While the Bible says we are called to be saints, when drawing near to God, we approach him with no credentials of our own; we have been given permission and access to "enter the holy places by the blood of Jesus." By the blood of Jesus!

Forbid it, Lord, that I should boast,
Save in the death of Christ my God![2]

An admirer of the late A. W. Tozer (1897-1963) once asked the highly esteemed preacher and author what his own position was regarding the centuries' old debate surrounding the differences between Arminianism and Calvinism on the subjects of salvation and sin. The venerable Doctor replied: "When I preach I'm an Arminian; when I pray, I'm a Calvinist." In other words, when Tozer preached, he preached a whosoever gospel; when he prayed, he prayed as a fallen, redeemed man. And that is how it should be.

A true heart doesn't try to impress God with its accomplishments, attainments, exploits, and successes—as though God can be impressed by such. No, the true-hearted believer draws near to God freely acknowledging his and her own foibles, failures in love, sins of commission and omission The true heart is honest with itself and with God. After all, only one man returned home justified before God in Jesus' parable in Luke 18—the man who cried out, "God be merciful to me, a sinner!" (v. 13).

The Second Key

The second essential key the writer holds out to believers in approaching God is "the full assurance of faith."

In contrast to the cautious circumspection with which the ancient

Jewish priests entered the tabernacle and temple to offer their sacrifices, the New Covenant believer has the high privilege of approaching God with great confidence.

This confidence is not to be confused with self-confidence. This inward persuasion that the writer calls "the full assurance of faith" is an attitude toward God that has been produced by the very Spirit of God in the believer's heart. Based on the authority of God's written record as well as having God's truth written on his heart and mind by the Holy Spirit, this believer is persuaded that God is real, that God hears and answers his prayers, and that his heavenly High Priest welcomes him and his petitions at the throne of mercy and grace. God says such a believer is to approach him with not only faith, nor merely an assurance of faith, but he and she are to come with "the full assurance of faith."

Regardless of our need—and we have many—we should not be reluctant in approaching God. Christ has opened a new and living way for us. The veil has been rent. Access to God has been perfected. Every redeemed sinner may now draw near to God—but let him do so with the full assurance of faith.

Since Christ's blood has been shed and since he has ascended on high to serve as our mediator, we can now approach God with the full assurance of faith as we offer our praises and thanksgivings, our petitions and supplications, our regrets and lamentations, our disappointments and bereavements, our aspirations and our dreams, our hurts and perplexities, our debts and trespasses.

With this in view, it is no wonder that the converted slave-trader of the eighteenth century, John Newton (1725-1807), should pen these words of full assurance:

> *Come, my soul, thy suit prepare;*
> *Jesus loves to answer prayer;*
> *He Himself has bid thee pray,*
> *Therefore will not say thee nay.*
>
> *Thou art coming to a King,*
> *Large petitions with thee bring;*
> *For His grace and pow'r are such*
> *None can ever ask too much.*[3]

Faith must be fed. Too many of us are starving our faith. We are spoiling our appetite for God by feasting on lesser things, not to say sinful things. Is it any wonder our faith is feeble? We pray with hardly a shred of confidence. There is no boldness in our praying; there is no heart-conviction that God our High Priest welcomes our intercessions — that we have One at the Father's right hand making intercession for us. If there are those who enjoy a greater intimacy with and a greater confidence in God than we do, it is because they take time to feed their faith, to feed it with the Word of God and the writings of godly men and women of faith.

To approach God in "the full assurance of faith" has been one of the marks that has characterized each of God's true servants. Such bold, confident faith produces results.

It reminds me of a remarkable incident from the life and ministry of the Evangelist Duncan Campbell (1898-1972). For several years, this Presbyterian ministered among his native people on the Hebrides Islands, off Scotland's coast.

At one period during the course of his itinerant ministry, Campbell was on the Island of Lewis, in a small village. Because of considerable opposition to his ministry and message, only seven people had come to the services in the local chapel. At the close of one of these disappointing services, the session-clerk of the congregation approached the minister and suggested that an all-night prayer meeting should be called. Campbell recounts what followed.

> So we met. There were about thirty of us, and prayer began. I found it a very hard meeting. I found myself battling and getting nowhere as the hours passed. After midnight between 12 and 1 o'clock in the morning, I turned to a young man in the meeting and said, "I feel led of God to ask you to pray," and that dear man rose to his feet and prayed, and in his prayer he uttered words such as I had never heard in a prayer before. He said, "Lord, You made a promise, are You going to fulfill it? We believe that You are a covenant-keeping God, will You be true to Your covenant? You have said that You would pour water on the thirsty and floods upon the dry ground. I do not know how others stand in Your Presence, I do not know how the ministers stand, but if I know my own heart, I know where I

stand, and I tell Thee now that I am thirsty, oh, I am thirsty for a manifestation of the Man of Thy right hand," —and then he said this—"Lord before I sit down, I want to tell You that Your honour is at stake."

Then Campbell added, "I love to believe that angels and archangels were looking over the battlements of Glory and saying to one another, 'This is a man who believes God, there is a man who dares to stand solid on the promise of God and take from the throne what the throne has promised.'"

Immediately following that prayer, Campbell said, "the community was alive with an awareness of God." Whereas there had only been seven people attending the services before, the Presbyterian evangelist records, "Men and women were carrying stools and chairs and asking, 'Is there room for us in the church'"[4]

Oh that we might approach our Father in Heaven in believing prayer "in the full assurance of faith." Faith unlocks Heaven's door.

The Third and Fourth Keys

The third and fourth keys we are to use in drawing near to God are the keys of a cleansed conscience and life: "Let us draw near with our hearts sprinkled clean from an evil conscience and our bodies washed with pure water."

Under the Old Covenant, Yahweh instructed Moses to use three material substances at their appointed time during a variety of worship experiences: blood, water, and oil. Allusions to two of these elements are made in this context—blood and water.

No doubt the sprinkling the writer has in view here is Israel's Day of Atonement. God instructs Moses that on that day the high priest is to enter the Holy of Holies and

> shall take some of the blood of the bull and sprinkle it with his finger on the front of the mercy seat on the east side, and in front of the mercy seat he shall sprinkle some of the blood with his finger seven times. Then he shall kill the goat of the sin offering that is for the people and bring its blood inside the veil and do with its blood as he did with the blood of the bull, sprinkling it over the mercy seat and in front of the mercy seat.

Thus he shall make atonement for the Holy Place, because of the uncleannesses of the people of Israel and because of their transgressions, all their sins (Lev. 16:14-16).

It was the above ritual, and the entire Azazel ceremony (Leviticus 16), that the writer of Hebrews had in mind when he wrote,

For if the blood of goats and bulls, and the sprinkling of defiled persons with the ashes of a heifer, sanctify for the purification of the flesh, how much more will the blood of Christ, who through the eternal Spirit offered himself without blemish to God, purify our conscience from dead works to serve the living God (Heb. 9:13-14).

After the sprinkling of blood and the Azazel ceremony, the high priest went through a washing ceremony:

Then Aaron shall come into the tent of meeting and shall take off the linen garments that he put on when he went into the Holy Place and shall leave them there. And he shall bathe his body in water in a holy place and put on his garments and come out and offer his burnt offering and the burnt offering of the people and make atonement for himself and for the people (Lev. 16:23-24).

The writer employs two perfect tense participles in this passage — more correctly rendered, "having been sprinkled" and "having been washed." As William Lane accurately notes, "These clauses have reference to the application of the benefits of Christ's sacrifice to the Christian at some decisive moment in the past. The perfect tenses of the participles refer to actions which are accomplished and enduring facts; they stress conditions of approach to God which Christians already enjoy."[5]

Here is the point the writer is making: for one to draw near to our holy God, proper preparation must take place. The believer is only qualified to approach God having had his conscience sprinkled with the blood of Christ and having had his body — representing his external conduct — purified.

Every believer knows such a sprinkling and washing occurred

when he and she first came to faith in Christ. But every honest believer also knows that he and she require fresh sprinklings, repeated sprinklings of the sacrificial benefits of the cleansing blood of Christ and the renewing of the Holy Spirit.

What should a Christian do when he fails in his walk with God? Despair? Rationalize his failure? Hide behind the mask of perfectionism? No! What is the advice of the inspired writer? "My little children, I am writing these things to you so that you may not sin. But if anyone does sin, we have an advocate with the Father, Jesus Christ the righteous. He is the propitiation for our sins, and not for ours only but also for the sins of the whole world" (1 John 2:1-2). John says Christ is the "propitiation for our sins." And again, "If we confess our sins, he is faithful and just to forgive us our sins and to cleanse us from all unrighteousness" (1 John 1:7).

Dr. Dennis Kinlaw writes, "There are some days when I know that I have not acted as I ought, when I have been more like the forlorn disciples on Easter night than I would like to admit. I can almost hear the heavenly Father ask Jesus, 'Son, how did that Kinlaw guy do today?' I hear the Son respond, 'Well, Father, he did not do so well today. . . .'" Kinlaw proceeds, "Then I hear the Father say, 'Shall we give up on him?' But then my spirit leaps . . . when, in my imagination, I see Jesus lift two scarred hands to the Father and say, 'No, Father. We have a substantial investment in him. We are not going to give up on him.'"[6] Dr. Kinlaw was merely practicing the above truth of the need for a renewed cleansing.

Dear believing reader, deep in your heart you have a desire to live close to God, to live in intimacy with your heavenly Father. Such a desire has been implanted by the Spirit of God. He invites you now to draw near—"Let us continually draw near"—in prayer and worship, in petition and supplication, in confession with contrition, in praise and thanksgiving.

On what basis do we have a right to draw near to God? The very blood of Jesus. What is to be our attitude and heart condition in preparing us to draw near to God; what are the keys in gaining an audience with the High and Holy One who inhabits eternity whose name is Holy? A true heart, full assurance of faith, a cleansed conscience and a purified life.

With such preparation, we can approach the holy throne crying . . . and sometimes singing,

> *With confidence I now draw nigh,*
> *And, "Father, Abba, Father," cry."*[7]

Let us draw near . . .

Drawing Near
(Part 3)

Ralph I. Tilley

There are three additional texts in the Letter to the Hebrews I wish to address in this chapter.

Hebrews 4:16

Let us then with confidence draw near to the throne of grace, that we may receive mercy and find grace to help in time of need.[1]

There are four explicit "throne" references in the book of Hebrews. This throne is called by the author the "throne of God" (1:8, 12:2), "the throne of the Majesty in the heaven" (8:1), and "the throne of grace" (4:16).

In speaking of this throne, the writer cites Psalm 45 and says the throne is eternal—"forever and ever"—and that God rules from this throne in righteousness: "the scepter of uprightness is the scepter of your kingdom" (see Heb. 1:8; Psa. 45:6-7). Furthermore, we are told twice by the writer that our heavenly High Priest is seated at the right hand of the throne—a position of prominence, honor, and authority (see Heb. 8:1; 12:2).

The term "throne" suggests an exalted position, royalty, rule, power, dignity, sovereignty. Inherent in the personhood of God are all of these attributes—and infinitely so much more. Isaiah saw in a vision "the Lord sitting upon a throne, high and lifted up" (Isa. 6:1). Moreover, he quotes God as saying, "I dwell in the high and holy place" (Isa. 57:15). As to the perpetuity of his reign and rulership, the Word of God repeatedly says, "The LORD is king forever and ever" (Psa. 10:16)[2]

The New Testament is replete with references to God's glorious throne, heavenly throne, God and the Lamb seated upon the throne, the throne of judgment, and eternal life flowing from the throne.[3] Implicit, of course, in all of Jesus' parables of the kingdom is the throne. With a kingdom there is a king; and with a king there is of necessity a throne.

Isn't the heart filled with Spirit-inspired gratitude when reflecting upon the sovereign rule of our Lord and God? How the hymnists of history extolled the reign of the almighty, eternal King! The words of the God-worshiping poet Robert Grant (1785-1838) are but a small sampling from a vast repertoire in Christian hymnody.

> *O worship the King, all glorious above,*
> *O gratefully sing His power and His love;*
> *Our Shield and Defender, the Ancient of Days,*
> *Pavilioned in splendor, and girded with praise.*[4]

Back to our text. The inspired writer of Hebrews calls this throne the believer is to approach with confidence "the throne of grace." Note, he did not call this throne the throne of law, nor did he call it the throne of judgment. He called it the throne of grace!

While Jesus made clear that the law of God was not destroyed by his coming,[5] and the Bible furthermore asserts that there is a future judgment for saints as well as for sinners,[6] the writer of Hebrews' emphasis in 4:16 is one of encouragement for spiritually weary and faint-hearted Christians—thus his reference to the throne as the throne of grace.

In the immediate context of 4:16, the writer has warned his readers against hardening their hearts and falling into disobedience, like the Israelites of old. God's word, he reminds them, is not static and sterile. Quite the contrary. He declares the Word is: "living and active, sharper than any two-edged sword, piercing to the division of soul and of spirit, of joints and of marrow, and discerning the thoughts and intentions of the heart. And no creature is hidden from his sight, but all are naked and exposed to the eyes of him to whom we must give account" (Heb. 4:12-13).

With such sober words before his readers, the writer wants to raise their spirits. So he transitions from warning to encouragement. In so many words, he encourages them to take hope. What is his basis for offering such encouragement? In contrast to a finite, temporal, outdated priesthood, he assures them, "we have a great high priest who has passed through the heavens, Jesus the Son of God." So instead of forfeiting your faith, because of discouragement, he says, "let us hold fast our confession" (Heb. 4:14).

These struggling believers were undoubtedly thinking at this point, *How will we make it? How can we possibly endure?* The writer's answer:

> For we do not have a high priest who is unable to sympathize with our weaknesses, but one who in every respect has been tempted as we are, yet without sin (Heb. 4:15).

This is precisely what they needed to hear. They needed sympathy! Why was that? Because they were in a real struggle. Some were in danger of apostasy (see 5:11-6:12). Some were on the verge of losing faith — of shrinking back and being spiritually destroyed (10:36-39). What were they encountering that caused such a struggle of faith? Great suffering, public exposure to reproach, ridicule, and affliction. Many of them even had their property plundered. Some were imprisoned (see 10:32-34) because of their Christian identity.

I wonder what prayer-request time sounded like in a first century prayer meeting. I have an idea it was unlike many of ours. Oh, the endless litany of inane requests one hears in today's prayer services! These early believers faced death. Their houses were ransacked. Their bodies were tortured. Their jobs were on the line. Many of their family and friends had deserted them. They no longer offered sacrifices at the Temple; they no longer accessed God through a Levitical priest; they no longer worshiped the way they once did. For this, they were mocked, beaten, slandered, ridiculed, imprisoned.

Some of these fledgling saints were turning back; some were on the verge of forsaking the faith. Many of them were totally discouraged. They were paying a big price to follow this crucified, risen, and ascended Lord.

These saints needed sympathy!

I imagine that a typical house church prayer request in the first century went something like this:

> Brothers and sisters, Naomi needs our prayers. She was beaten on her way home from working in the harvest fields last evening. That's why you don't see her here tonight. As you know, we were excommunicated from the synagogue last week because of our public confession of faith in Jesus as our risen Lord and Savior. Our young children are grievously distraught over what happened to their mother. To compound their plight, they have lost all their friends at synagogue. I hate to burden you with more, but I was informed three days ago by my employer that he will dismiss me from a position I have held for more than fifteen years if I don't publicly renounce Jesus Christ as Lord.

These believers were weak and vulnerable; they were tempted to turn back. What a welcome word of encouragement they heard when this letter was read in their meetings: "For we do not have a high priest who is unable to sympathize with our weaknesses, but one who in every respect has been tempted as we are, yet without sin" (Heb. 4:15).

The writer doesn't write, "For we did not have a high priest who is unable to sympathize with our weaknesses, but one . . ." No, he wrote quite the contrary: "For we do not have a high priest who is unable to sympathize with our weaknesses, but one who in every respect has been tempted as we are, yet without sin."

Do you see the difference? The bold affirmation is this: "FOR WE DO HAVE A HIGH PRIEST WHO IS ABLE TO SYMPATHIZE WITH OUR WEAKNESSES!"

One of the qualifications for a person to be a high priest under the Levitical law was that he should possess the capacity to deal sympathetically with the worshipers: "He can deal gently with the ignorant and wayward, since he himself is beset with weakness" (Heb. 5:2).

The priests did not always live up to their high calling. New Testament scholar F. F. Bruce noted, "from the fall of the house of Zadok [171 B.C.] to the destruction of the temple [70 A.D.] two hundred and forty years later there were very few high priests in Israel who manifested the personal qualities so indispensable to their sacred office."[7]

The author of Hebrews says the priests under the Old Covenant were compelled to deal sympathetically with the people because they themselves were "beset with weakness." However, Jesus sympathizes with our weakness (so says the writer) — not because he himself was weak — he wasn't — but because he underwent temptation, just like we do.

The writer declares that contemporaneous with the suffering these Hebrew Christians were experiencing, their ever-living High Priest, Jesus Christ, was sympathizing with them — right then and there. He's on his heavenly throne to be sure, but he also dwells within them by his Spirit. Space is no factor for the living Christ, who transcends all space and time.

New Testament Greek scholar B. F. Westcott (1825-1901) remarks on the Greek word translated "sympathize": "It expresses not simply the compassion of one who regards suffering from without, but the feeling of one who enters into the suffering and makes it his own."[8] The noun form of the word is found in Hebrews 10:34 and 1 Peter 3:8 and translated as compassion and sympathy: "For you had compassion on those in prison" and "Finally, all of you, have . . . sympathy." An excellent English equivalent is the word empathy — meaning identification with and understanding of another's situation, feelings, etc.

The writer says that our heavenly High Priest is able to sympathize with us because of our "weaknesses." What are these weaknesses he makes reference to? The next chapter surely provides us with at least a partial answer to our question. I previously cited Hebrews 5:2; here I will include verse 3 as well. The writer is speaking about the high priests under the Old Covenant:

> He can deal gently with the ignorant and wayward, since he himself is beset with weakness. Because of this he is obligated to offer sacrifice for his own sins just as he does for those of the people.

In 4:15 the writer speaks of "our weaknesses" — something that he himself and all his readers experienced. In 5:2 he associates "weakness" with "the ignorant and wayward." Bruce suggests, "we should understand a hendiadys [a figure of speech in which two words connected with a conjunction are used to express a single notion] here and take the phrase to mean 'those who go astray through ignorance.'"[9] We know from the book of Leviticus that God prescribed specific sacrifices to be offered by those who had sinned in ignorance or unintentionally.[10] Such acts were considered "unintentional" because the transgressor was uninformed about a specific religious or moral duty that God had previously announced. It was considered "sin," even though it was unintentional, because the transgression violated God's holy law and will. There were no prescribed sacrifices for intentional sins, or what Numbers calls sins committed with a "high hand": "But the person who does anything with a high hand, whether he is native or a sojourner, reviles the LORD, and that person shall be cut off from among his people" (Num. 15:30).

While the "weaknesses" include unintentional sins, it is much broader. New Testament scholar Craig Koester correctly notes the writer of Hebrews warns against such highhanded sins (e.g., apostasy in chapter 6). But he also observes that the epistle makes no distinction between voluntary and involuntary sins. "Christ atoned for all sins, both voluntary and involuntary."[11] Including all the sins of every follower of Jesus: "He is the propitiation for our sins, and not for ours only but also for the sins of the whole world" (1 John 2:1-2).

While the high priest under the Old Covenant was able to deal gently with the ignorant and wayward, since he himself was beset with weaknesses (note Aaron as one example), the writer says that Jesus — our heavenly High Priest — is qualified to sympathize with our weaknesses because he is "one who in every respect has been tempted as we are, yet without sin."

Jesus is able to sympathize with us — not because he sinned — but because he himself was tempted. In other words, because Jesus felt and experienced the full force of temptation while here on earth — actually "suffered when tempted" (Heb. 2:18) — he is able to sympathize with all of his followers who are being tempted.

God has no sympathy for sin. But he has infinite sympathy for us in our temptations and, praise be to God, even when we have failed in our temptations . . . there is mercy. One notable example: "Simon, Simon, behold, Satan demanded to have you, that he might sift you like wheat, but I have prayed for you that your faith may not fail. And when you have turned again, strengthen your brothers" (Lk. 22:31-32).

Timely grace is what I need when facing each and every temptation. Mercy is what I need when I've failed to appropriate available grace. Simon Peter received mercy when he miserably failed the Lord Jesus Christ. Kind David received mercy when he fell into sexual sin. Joseph appropriated grace to enable him to flee from temptation. Daniel appropriated grace to enable him to be faithful in a strange land.

Yes, God's intention for us is that we not fail. But God, mercifully, has provided for us when we do fail. Not only did Jesus die once for sin; he presently intercedes for us as our High Priest and Advocate to administer mercy and grace. Since this is so, God encouragingly says to us "Let us keep on coming to the throne of grace, that we may receive mercy and find grace to help in time of need."

How I love the poetic words of Methodism's sweet hymnist on this subject. While legions of his and his brother's followers have rigorously promulgated a form of sinless perfectionism, Charles Wesley (1707-1788) knew better. In these words he offered hope to the Christian who failed — and who among us has not?

> *Whence to me this waste of love?*
> *Ask my Advocate above!*
> *See the cause in Jesus' face,*
> *Now before the throne of grace.*
>
> *There for me the Savior stands,*
> *Shows His wounds and spreads His hands.*
> *God is love! I know, I feel;*
> *Jesus weeps and loves me still.*[12]

Yes, by all means call upon the Lord for grace in time of need; however, when overcome with weakness — call upon him for mercy. After all, the throne we are to continually approach with confidence is called by God himself the "throne of grace"! Let us draw near . . .

Drawing Near
(Part 4)

Ralph I. Tilley

William Kirkpatrick (1838-1921) was a prolific poet and hymn writer, as well as an accomplished church organist. Of his many published songs, there is one I remember often singing, especially during the formative years of my Christian journey: "Saved to the Uttermost." I can still hear the refrain of this song ringing in my ears even now many years later:

> *Saved, saved, saved to the uttermost!*
> *Saved, saved by power divine!*
> *Saved, saved, saved to the uttermost!*
> *Jesus, the Saviour, is mine*[1]

The theme of Kirkpatrick's song is taken from a word found in Hebrews 7:25. For the purposes of this part in this "Drawing Near" series, let's place that verse in its context:

> The former priests were many in number, because they were prevented by death from continuing in office, but he holds his priesthood permanently, because he continues forever. Consequently, he is able to save to the uttermost those who draw near to God through him, since he always lives to make intercession for them.[2]

God is Able

What does the writer mean by the phrase "he is able to save to the uttermost those who draw near to God through him"?

First, let's take a look at the phrase "he is able."

The truth of this phrase has brought great blessing to the people of God across the ages. The omnipotence of God is wrapped up in this powerful affirmation. The New Testament writers provide a host of examples and promises concerning God's infinite, multifaceted abilities as they relate to believers. For example:

• Abraham believed "God was able to do what he had promised."

• Nothing "will be able to separate us from the love of God in Christ Jesus our Lord."

• To the generous Corinthians: "God is able to make all grace abound to you, so that having all sufficiency in all things at all times, you may abound in every good work."

• Paul concludes his prayer in Ephesians 3 with these reassuring words: "Now to him who is able to do far more abundantly than all that we ask or think, according to the power at work within us, . . ."

• To the tempted: "For because he himself has suffered when tempted, he is able to help those who are being tempted."

• To those who fear they might fail to finish the Christian race: "Now to him who is able to keep you from stumbling and to present you blameless before the presence of his glory with great joy."[3]

It has now been over forty-five years since I first read the following words from the pen of one of English Methodism's saintly preachers and educators. In my copy of the book, that is now taped and held together by a rubber band because of frequent use, Thomas Cook (1859-1913) said of God's promises: "every promise is built upon four pillars, each one as strong as the pillars of Heaven—God's justice or holiness, which will not suffer him to deceive; His grace and goodness, which will not suffer Him to forget; His truth, which will not suffer Him to change; and His power, which makes Him able to accomplish."[4]

Oh, the immensity and intensity of the promises of God given to thirsty-hearted believers! How can we ever doubt them; how can we ever doubt him? Do we really believe "he is able to save to the uttermost those who draw near to God through him"?

God is Able to Save

The Hebrews' writer declares: "he is able to save."

Speaking to the bewildered Joseph, the angel announced, "She will bear a son, and you shall call his name Jesus, for he will save his people from their sins" (Matt. 1:21). The Greek word for Jesus (*Iēsous*) in Hebrew is *Yeshua/Yehoshua* (Joshua), meaning "Yahweh saves." The first Joshua was a prototype of the second Joshua, the Lord Jesus Christ. As the successor to Moses brought great deliverance and victory to Israel, so the second Joshua—the "Long Expected Jesus"—brought salvation to Adam's entire race. The second Joshua came with the express purpose to seek and to save the lost. He came to save the prodigals and the profligates, the self-righteous and the unrighteous. The Lord Jesus welcomed the enquiring, astute Nicodemus as well as the tormented demon-possessed Gadarene. He sought out the educated, blasphemous Saul of Tarsus as well as a Samaritan woman who had gone from one marriage to another.

Jesus came to save—no matter our past or present. Jesus is able to save!

God is Able to Save Completely

The writer says Jesus "is able to save to the uttermost." The Greek phrase translated "to the uttermost" by the English Standard Version and King James Version is rendered as follows by other versions:

- "completely" (NIV, REB)
- "absolutely" (NEB)
- "forever" (NASB)
- "once and forever" (NLT)

What shall we make of this phrase?

The question asked by Bible students of this verse is, Should this phrase be understood in a temporal or qualitative sense? In other words, does the writer have in mind salvation as it relates to time or extent? The *ESV Study Bible* suggests that it can mean either or both:

> "To the uttermost" does not specify whether completeness in time ("forever") or completeness in extent ("completely") is intended; the Greek *eis to panteles* can mean both. Since a "complete" salvation would endure for all time, and since a salvation "for all time" would eventually include every aspect of life, perhaps the author intends readers to hear both senses.[5]

I fully agree with the above; only I would be inclined to drop the "perhaps."

New Testament scholar Craig Koester similarly agrees with the *ESV Study Bible* while wording it differently. He notes: "In a temporal sense *panteles* can mean 'for all time' so that it is synonymous with 'forever' (7:24b), 'always' (7:25b), and 'to all eternity.' In a qualitative sense the word can mean 'completely' so that it refers to 'complete salvation.'"[6]

We can then logically conclude that God's plan of salvation, as revealed in his written Word, includes salvation in the sense of completeness as to its extent ("completely"): salvation from sin's guilt and from sin's pollution. It also includes salvation in the sense of completeness as to time ("forever"): an eternal salvation which ultimately results in the deliverance from the very environment of sin.

As to salvation in the sense of completeness in extent, note this example (we need go no further than Hebrews): "how much more will the blood of Christ, who through the eternal Spirit offered himself without blemish to God, purify our conscience from dead works to serve the living God" (Heb. 9:14). As to salvation in the sense of completeness in time, note this example: "And being made perfect, he became the source of eternal salvation to all who obey him . . ." (Heb. 5:9).

Our Permanent Priest

One of the reasons the writer of Hebrews gives for Christ's ability to save his people completely and forever is because of his continuing, perpetual, and permanent priesthood, in contrast to the mortal priest-hood under the Old Covenant: "The former priests were many in number, because they were prevented by death from continuing in office, but he holds his priesthood permanently, because he continues forever. Consequently, he is able to save" (Heb. 7:23).

The Jewish historian Josephus (37-100) estimated there were a total of eighty-three high priests who served from Aaron to the destruction of temple worship in 70 A.D.[7] In addition to the high priests, there were thousands of other priests who performed lesser duties. Every one of these priests died; therefore he was prevented from continuing to exercise his priestly duties.

Not so with Jesus: "he holds his priesthood permanently, because he continues forever." Think of it: "permanently," "continues forever"!

Yes, our High Priest continues forever —
No mortal is He;
Permanently seated in the heavens,
Jesus pleads for me![8]

Drawing Near Through the Interceding Jesus

Who is it that Jesus is able to save completely and forever? —"those who draw near to God through him." With all due respect (and I mean this sincerely and charitably) to my Roman Catholic friends, the writer does not say that Jesus is able to save completely and forever those who draw near to God through Mary the mother of Jesus, nor through any other of the saintly dead who have gone on to their reward. While it is the privilege for all Christians to intercede for others, it is only one Mediator who sits in the presence of God the Father who makes all other intercessions effective—Jesus the crucified, risen, and ascended Lord and High Priest. In the words of the apostle: "For there is one God, and there is one mediator between God and men, the man Christ Jesus (1 Tim. 2:5).

This is no ordinary Mediator and Intercessor. F. F. Bruce (1910-1990) noted: "He is a unique Mediator between God and man because He combines Godhead and manhood perfectly in His own person; in Him God draws near to men and in Him men may draw near to God, with the assurance of constant and immediate access."[9] What a timely encouragement this would have been for these first-century believers when they heard this read to them.

Christ died once in order to purchase, provide, and secure our complete salvation: "he entered once for all into the holy places, not by means of the blood of goats and calves but by means of his own blood, thus securing an eternal redemption" (Heb. 9:12). Christ is able to completely and forever save his people "since he always lives to make intercession for them."

Let me say this reverently: The atoning death and resurrection of Christ were insufficient events in and of themselves to *sustain* our salvation. In the wisdom of God, he deemed it necessary for his Son to perform a continuing ministry of intercession for his church in order to ensure *complete* and *final* salvation for all true believers.

The atoning death and resurrection of Jesus Christ will never be repeated; they were once-for-all salvific events, however with eternal implications. Yes, the intercessory ministry of the Lord Jesus as our High Priest will continue until the Church Militant becomes the Church Triumphant:

Till all the ransomed church of God be saved, to sin no more"[10]

And no doubt even then the Church Triumphant will still be in need of their continuing Intercessor.

There is one particular encounter during Jesus' earthly ministry that helps us to understand his current intercessory ministry. We have an account in Luke 22 where Jesus foretold Simon Peter of the disciple's imminent three-fold denial, But with his prediction, Jesus provides Peter with a wonderful word of encouragement: "but I have prayed for you that your faith may not fail" (Luke 22:32). Peter would fail—and fail miserably—but his failure would not be final: "I have prayed for you." In commenting on this text, Bruce says, "If it be asked what form His heavenly intercession takes, what better answer can be given than that He still does for his people at the right hand of God what He did for Peter on earth?"[11]

As to the mode of Jesus' intercessions, Bruce cites H. B. Swete's (1835-1917) insightful comments: Jesus "is not to be thought as an orante, standing ever before the Father with outstretched arms, like the figures in the mosaics of catacombs, . . . but as a throned Priest-King, asking what He will from a Father who always hears and grants His request."[12] In the words of one of Christendom's most highly regarded hymnists:

> *He ever lives above*
> *For me to intercede,*
> *His all-redeeming love,*
> *His precious blood to plead.*[13]

Yes, it is the continuing intercessions of the Lord Jesus Christ, the Christian's high Priest at the Father's right hand, which secures and sustains our salvation. Without the prayers of Jesus, Peter's failure would have been final. And without the heavenly intercessions of the Lord Jesus, each of us likewise would live defeated lives and finally fail and be lost forever. But—hallelujah!—"he is able to save to the uttermost those who draw near to God through him, since he always lives to make intercession for them."

Dear reader, let us draw near to God today and every day—and often throughout the day—in then name of our interceding High Priest, the Lord Jesus Christ. Let us bring our thanksgivings and adorations, our petitions and intercessions. Let us bring our own needs, as well as those of others. By all means, let us pray—pray regularly and fervently pray with confidence and persistently. Remember, our Father in heaven awaits to listen to the sincere cries of his children, and delights in answering their requests.

Let us draw near . . .

23

This Spirit of Supplication

Andrew Murray

> *"I will pour upon the house of David the Spirit*
> *of grace and of supplication."*
> — Zechariah 12:10

> *"The Spirit also helpeth our infirmity; for we know not how to pray as*
> *we ought: but the Spirit Himself maketh intercession for us with*
> *groanings which cannot be uttered. And He that searcheth the*
> *hearts knoweth what is the mind of the Spirit, because He maketh*
> *intercession for the saints according to God."*
> — Romans 8:26-27

> *"With all prayer and supplication praying at all*
> *seasons in the Spirit, and watching thereunto in all*
> *perseverance and supplication for all the saints."*
> — Ephesians 6:18

> *"Praying in the Holy Spirit."*
> — Jude 20

The Holy Spirit has been given to every child of God to be his life. He dwells in him, not as a separate Being in one part of his nature, but as his very life. He is the Divine power or energy by which his life is maintained and strengthened. All that a believer is called to be or to do, the Holy Spirit can and will work in him. If he does not know or yield to the Holy Guest, the blessed Spirit cannot work, and his life is a sickly

The second lesson is: Beware above everything of grieving the Holy Spirit (Eph. 4:30). If you do, how can he work in you the quiet, trustful, and blessed sense of that union with Christ which makes your prayers well-pleasing to the Father? Beware of grieving him by sin, by unbelief, by selfishness, by unfaithfulness to his voice in conscience. Do not think grieving him a necessity: that cuts away the very sinews of your strength. Do not consider it impossible to obey the command, "Grieve not the Holy Spirit." He himself is the very power of God to make you obedient. The sin that comes up in you against your will, the tendency to sloth, or pride, or self-will, or passion that rises in the flesh, your will can, in the power of the Spirit, at once reject, and cast upon Christ and his blood, and your communion with God is immediately restored. Accept each day the Holy Spirit as your Leader and Life and Strength; you can count upon Him to do in your heart all that ought to be done there. He, the Unseen and Unfelt One, but known by faith, gives there, unseen and unfelt, the love and the faith and the power of obedience you need, because he reveals Christ unseen within you, as actually your Life and Strength. Grieve not the Holy Spirit by distrusting him, because you do not feel his presence in you.

Especially in the matter of prayer, grieve him not. Do not expect, when you trust Christ to bring you into a new, healthy prayer-life, that you will be able all at once to pray as easily and powerfully and joyfully as you would wish. No, it may not come at once. But just bow quietly before God in your ignorance and weakness. That is the best and truest prayer, to put yourself before God just as you are, and to count on the hidden Spirit praying in you. "We know not what to pray as we ought"; ignorance, difficulty, struggle, marks our prayer all along. But, "the Spirit helpeth our infirmities." How? "The Spirit himself," deeper down than our thoughts or feelings, "maketh intercession for us with groanings which cannot be uttered." When you cannot find words, when your words appear cold and feeble, just believe: The Holy Spirit is praying in me. Be quiet before God, and give him time and opportunity; in due season you will learn to pray. Beware of grieving the Spirit of prayer, by not honouring Him in patient, trustful surrender to his intercession in you.

The third lesson: "Be filled with the Spirit" (Eph. 5:18). I think that one, full of failure and of sin. As he yields, and waits, and obeys the leading of the Spirit, God works in him all that is pleasing in his sight.

This Holy Spirit is, in the first place, a Spirit of prayer. He was promised as a "Spirit of grace and supplication," the grace for supplication. He was sent forth into our hearts as "the Spirit of adoption, whereby we cry, Abba, Father." He enables us to say, in true faith and growing apprehension of its meaning, "Our Father which art in Heaven." "He maketh intercession for the saints according to the will of God." And as we pray in the Spirit, our worship is as God seeks it to be, "in spirit and in truth." Prayer is just the breathing of the Spirit in us; power in prayer comes from the power of the Spirit in us, waited on and trusted in. Failure in prayer comes from feebleness of the Spirit's work in us. Our prayer is the index of the measure of the Spirit's work in us. To pray aright, the life of the Spirit must be right in us. For praying the effectual, much-availing prayer of the righteous man, everything depends on being full of the Spirit.

There are three very simple lessons that the believer, who would enjoy the blessing of being taught to pray by the Spirit of prayer, must know.

The first lesson is: Believe that the Spirit dwells in you (Eph. 1:13). Deep in the inmost recesses of his being, hidden and unfelt, every child of God has the Holy, Mighty Spirit of God dwelling in him. He knows it by faith, the faith that, accepting God's Word, realizes that of which he sees as yet no sign. "We receive the promise of the Spirit by faith." As long as we measure our power, for praying aright and perseveringly, by what we feel, or think we can accomplish, we shall be discouraged when we hear of how much we ought to pray. But when we quietly believe that, in the midst of all our conscious weakness, the Holy Spirit as a Spirit of supplication is dwelling within us, for the very purpose of enabling us to pray in such manner and measure as God would have us, our hearts will be filled with hope. We shall be strengthened in the assurance which lies at the very root of a happy and fruitful Christian life, that God has made an abundant provision for our being what he wants us to be. We shall begin to lose our sense of burden and fear and discouragement about praying sufficiently, because we see that the Holy Spirit himself will pray, is praying, in us.

we have seen the meaning of the great truth: It is only the healthy spiritual life that can pray aright. The command comes to each of us: "Be filled with the Spirit." That implies that while some rest content with the beginning, with a small measure of the Spirit's working, it is God's will that we should be filled with the Spirit. That means, from our side, that our whole being ought to be entirely yielded up to the Holy Spirit, to be possessed and controlled by him alone. And, from God's side, that we may count upon and expect the Holy Spirit to take possession and fill us. Has not our failure in prayer evidently been owing to our not having accepted the Spirit of prayer to be our life; to our not having yielded wholly to him, whom the Father gave as the Spirit of his Son, to work the life of the Son in us? Let us, to say the very least, be willing to receive him, to yield ourselves to God and trust him for it. Let us not again willfully grieve the Holy Spirit by declining, by neglecting, by hesitating to seek to have him as fully as he is willing to give himself to us. If we have at all seen that prayer is the great need of our work and of the Church, if we have at all desired or resolved to pray more, let us turn to the very source of all power and blessing—let us believe that the Spirit of prayer, even in his fullness, is for us.

We all admit the place the Father and the Son have in our prayer. It is to the Father we pray, and from whom we expect the answer. It is in the merit, and name, and life of the Son, abiding in him and he in us, that we trust to be heard. But have we understood that in the Holy Trinity all the Three Persons have an equal place in prayer, and that the faith in the Holy Spirit of intercession as praying in us is as indispensable as the faith in the Father and the Son? How clearly we have this in the words, "Through Christ we have access by one Spirit to the Father" (Eph. 2:18). As much as prayer must be to the Father, and through the Son, it must be by the Spirit. And the Spirit can pray in no other way in us, than as he lives in us. It is only as we give ourselves to the Spirit living and praying in us, that the glory of the prayer-hearing God, and the ever-blessed and most effectual mediation of the Son, can be known by us in their power.

Our last lesson: "Pray in the Spirit for all saints" (Eph. 6:18). The Spirit, who is called "the Spirit of supplication," is also and very specially the Spirit of intercession. It is said of him, "the Spirit himself maketh intercession for us with groanings that cannot be uttered." "He maketh intercession for the saints." It is the same word as is used of Christ, "who also maketh intercession for us." The thought is essentially that of *mediation*—one pleading for another. When the Spirit of intercession takes full possession of us, all selfishness, as if we wanted him separate from his intercession for others, and have him for ourselves alone, is banished, and we begin to avail ourselves of our wonderful privilege to plead for men. We long to live the Christ-life of self-consuming sacrifice for others, as our heart unceasingly yields itself to God to obtain his blessing for those around us. Intercession then becomes, not an incident or an occasional part of our prayers, but their one great object. Prayer for ourselves then takes its true place, simply as a means for fitting us better for exercising our ministry of intercession more effectually.

May I be allowed to speak a very personal word to each of my readers? I have humbly besought God to give me what I may give them—Divine light and help truly to forsake the life of failure in prayer, and to enter, even now, and at once, upon the life of intercession which the Holy Spirit can enable them to lead. It can be done by a simple act of faith, claiming the fullness of the Spirit, that is, the full measure of the Spirit which you are capable in God's sight of receiving, and he is therefore willing to bestow. Will you not, even now, accept of this by faith?

Let me remind you of what takes place at conversion. Most of us, you probably too, for a time sought peace in efforts and struggles to give up sin and please God. But you did not find it thus. The peace of God's pardon came by faith, trusting God's Word concerning Christ and his salvation. You had heard of Christ as the gift of his love, you knew that he was for you too, you had felt the movings and drawings of his grace; but never till in faith in God's Word you accepted him as God's gift to you, did you know the peace and joy that he can give. Believing in him and his saving love made all the difference, and changed your relation from one who had ever grieved him, to one who loved and served him. And yet, after a time, you have a thousand times wondered that you love and serve him so ill.

At the time of your conversion you knew little about the Holy Spirit. Later on you heard of his dwelling in you, and his being the power

137

of God in you for all the Father intends you to be, and yet his indwelling and in-working have been something vague and indefinite, and hardly a source of joy or strength. At conversion you did not yet know your need of him, and still less what you might expect of him. But your failures have taught it you. And now you begin to see how you have been grieving him, by not trusting and not following him, by not allowing him to work in you all God's pleasure.

All this can be changed. Just as you, after seeking Christ, and praying to him, and trying without success to serve him, found rest in accepting him by faith, just so you may even now yield yourself to the full guidance of the Holy Spirit, and claim and accept him to work in you what God would have. Will you not do it? Just accept him in faith as Christ's gift, to be the Spirit of your whole life, of your prayer-life too, and you can count upon him to take charge. You can then begin, however feeble you feel, and unable to pray aright, to bow before God in silence, with the assurance that he will teach you to pray.

My dear brother and sister, as you consciously by faith accepted Christ, to pardon, you can consciously now in the like faith accept of Christ who gives the Holy Spirit to do his work in you. Christ redeemed us that we might receive the promise of the Spirit by faith. Kneel down, and simply believe that the Lord Christ, who baptizes with the Holy Spirit, does now, in response to your faith, begin in you the blessed life of a full experience of the power of the indwelling Spirit. Depend most confidently upon him, apart from all feeling or experience, as the Spirit of supplication and intercession to do his work. Renew that act of faith each morning, each time you pray; trust him, against all appearances, to work in you—be sure he is working,—and he will give you to know what the joy of the Holy Spirit is as the power of your life.

"I will pour out the Spirit of supplication." Do you not begin to see that the mystery of prayer is the mystery of the Divine indwelling. God in Heaven gives his Spirit in our hearts to be there the Divine power praying in us, and drawing us upward to our God. God is a Spirit, and nothing but a like life and Spirit within us can hold communion with him. It was for this man was created, that God might dwell and work in him, and be the life of his life. It was this Divine indwelling that sin lost. It was this that Christ came to exhibit in his life, to win back for us in his death, and then to impart to us by coming again from Heaven in the Spirit to live in his disciples. It is this, the indwelling of God through the Spirit, that alone can explain and enable us to appropriate the wonderful promises given to prayer. God gives the Spirit as a Spirit of Supplication, too, to maintain his Divine life within us as a life out of which prayer ever rises upward.

Without the Holy Spirit no man can call Jesus Lord, or cry, Abba, Father; no man can worship in spirit and truth, or pray without ceasing. The Holy Spirit is given to the believer to be and do in him all that God wants him to be or do. He is given him especially as the Spirit of prayer and supplication. Is it not clear that everything in prayer depends upon our trusting the Holy Spirit to do his work in us; yielding ourselves to his leading, depending only and wholly on him?

We read, "Stephen was a man full of faith and the Holy Spirit" (Acts 6:5). The two ever go together, in exact proportion to each other. As our faith sees and trusts the Spirit in us to pray, and waits on him, he will do his work; and it is the longing desire, and the earnest supplication, and the definite faith the Father seeks. Do let us know him, and in the faith of Christ who unceasingly gives him, cultivate the assured confidence, we can learn to pray as the Father would have us.[1]

The Prayer Life of
George Whitefield

Edited by Ralph I. Tilley

The following selections are taken from George Whitefield's Journals, *1738. The opening paragraphs serve as his introduction to the main part of the Journals.*[1]

I began to read the Holy Scriptures upon my knees, laying aside all other books, and praying over, if possible, every line and word. This proved to be meat indeed, to my soul. I daily received fresh life, light, and power from above. I got more true knowledge from reading the Book of God in one month, than I could *ever* have acquired from all the writings of men. In one word, I found it profitable for reproof, for correction, for instruction in righteousness, every way sufficient to make the man of God perfect, thoroughly furnished unto every good word and work.

The shyness that Moses and some other prophets expressed, when God sent them out in a public capacity, I thought was sufficient to teach me not to run [i.e., become an ordained minister in the Church of England] till I was called. He Who knoweth the hearts of men, is witness that I never prayed more earnestly against entering anything than I did against entering into the service of the Church *so soon* [he was twenty years of age at the time]. Oftentimes I have been in an agony in prayer, when under convictions of my insufficiency for so great a work. With strong crying and tears I have often said, "Lord, I am a youth of uncircumcised lips; Lord, send me not into Thy vineyard yet."

Early in the morning, at noonday, evening, and at midnight, nay, all the day long, did the blessed Jesus visit and refresh my heart. Could the trees of a certain wood near Stonehouse speak, they would tell what sweet communion I and some others enjoyed with the ever blessed God there. Sometimes, as I was walking, my soul would make such sallies as though it would go out of the body. At other times, I would be so overpowered with a sense of God's Infinite Majesty, that I would be constrained to throw myself on the ground, and offer my soul as a blank in His hands, to write on it what He leased. One night, was a time never to be forgotten. It happened to lighten [lightning] exceedingly. I had been expounding to many people and some being afraid to go home, I thought it my duty to accompany them, and improve the occasion, to stir them up to prepare for the coming of the Son of Man. In my return to the parsonage house, whilst others were rising from their beds, frightened almost to death, I and another, a poor, but pious countryman, were in the field, exulting in our God, and longing for that time, when Jesus should be revealed from heaven in a flame of fire! Oh that my soul may be in a like frame, when He shall actually come to call me! For I think I never had been happier than that night, or, all things considered, more blessed than during my abode at Stonehouse.

The tide of popularity now began to run very high. In a short time I could no longer walk on foot as usual, but was constrained to go in a coach, from place to lace, to avoid the hosannas of the multitude. They grew quite extravagant in the applauses; and, had it not been for my compassionate High Priest, popularity would have destroyed me. I used to lead with Him, to take me by the hand and lead me unhurt through this fiery furnace. He heard my request, and gave me to see the vanity of all commendations but His own.

I had a sweet knot of religious friends, with whom I at first attempted to pray *extempore*. Some time, I think in October, we began to set apart an hour every evening, to intercede with the Great Head of the Church to carry on the work begun, and for the circle of our acquaintance, according as we knew their circumstances required. I was their mouth unto God, and He only knows what enlargement I felt in that Divine employ. Once we spent a whole night in prayer and praise; and many a time, at midnight and at one in the morning, after I have been wearied almost to death in preaching, writing, and conversation, and going from place to place, God imparted new life to my soul, and enabled me to intercede with Him for an hour-and-a-half and two hours together. The sweetness of this exercise made me compose my sermon upon "Intercession," and I cannot think it presumption to suppose that partly, at least, in answer to prayers then put up by His dear children, the Word, for some years past, has run and been glorified, not only in England, but in many other parts of the world.

Thousands and thousands of prayers were put up for me. They would run and stop me in the alleys, hug me in their arms, and follow me with wishful looks. Once in the Christmas before my departure [to America], with many others, I spent a night in prayer and praise . . .

1738 . . .

January 16. Mr. H. and I joined in an hour's intercession and abstinence, with all those who meet together to bewail their own and the sins of the nation.

January 21. At night, the number of my hearers was so increased, that the stairs were full, as well as my room. I expounded to them the 25th of St. Matthew; at which they were much affected, and seemed to love and pray for me most earnestly. I desire to have no greater portion than the prayers of the poor.

January 27. Spent the morning agreeably in conversation, intercession for all friends and all mankind, walking on the seashore.

February 3. Let this day be noted in my book, for God wrought for us a wonderful deliverance! About seven in the morning, the men upon decks not keeping a good look-out, one of the East India ships in shifting to the wind ran near us so very briskly, that had not Captain Whiting providentially been on deck, and beseeched them for God's sake to tack about, both the ships must inevitably have split one against another. They were within four yards of each other. The Captain said he never was in so great danger in his life. Mr. Habersham and I knew nothing of it till it was over; but when I was apprised of it, I endeavoured to excite all to thankfulness, and returned public thanks at prayers. Too many seemed to be insensible of the mercy received. But,

Since God does thus His wondrous love
Through all our lives extend;
Those lives to Him let us devote,
And in His service spend.

February 5. Joined in spirit with absent friends in holy ordinances; spent time most delightfully in reading the Word of God; read prayers, and made some observations on both Lessons to the soldiers. O that the Lord would open our understandings! for they are but a dead letter without the illumination of His Holy Spirit.

February 24. Blessed be God! Who this day hath shewn me that He hath heard my prayer, and not taken His lovingkindness from me. Long before I reached Gibraltar, I prayed that God would open an effectual door at the place whither we were going, and direct me where I should lodge, and lo! this day He has answered me. About ten in the morning came Capt. Mackay on board, telling me that one Major S. (a person I never saw), had provided me a convenient lodging at one merchant B's, and desired that I should come on shore. I looking upon this as a call from Providence, received it with all thankfulness and went with friend Habersham on shore, first praying that God would direct us how to behave.

About the middle of the town, Major S. gave us the meeting, conducted us to our new lodgings, which were very commodious, and engaged us to dine with him and Capt. Mackay. "When I sent you without scrip or shoes, lacked ye anything?" And they said, "Nothing, Lord!"

About eleven I was introduced by Doctor C. to General Columbine, who was desirous of seeing me. He received me exceeding kindly; and after a little serious conversation, we went to Governor Sabine's, and from thence to public prayers. I was highly pleased to see so many officers attending on the Generals to church. Doctor C. told me he had not known Governor Sabine absent himself from prayers once these several years, except when he was hindered by sickness. Oh that all others would let their light so shine before men!

Retired in the evening to our lodgings. Had family prayer, wrote some few religious letters, and spent near half-an-hour in serious conversation with the people of the house, and was soon convinced that God had sent me to that particular lodging of a truth. "Be careful for nothing; but in every (even the minutest) thing, make your wants known unto God." "For He careth for you."

March 1. Expounded in the morning,, and was pleased at my entrance into the church, to see several soldiers kneeling in several parts of the House of God at their private devotions. O happy Gibraltar, that thou hast such a set of praying men! Some I hear, often come in by two o'clock in the morning, to pour our their hearts before God. The Lord perform all their petitions!

March 4. Went in the afternoon to the Jewish synagogue, and was surprised to see one of the head of them come from the farthest end, and put me in one of their chiefest seats. But afterwards he told me he had heard my sermon yesterday against swearing, and thanked me for it. I continued with them their whole service, and spent most of my time there in secret prayer to God that the veil might be taken from their hearts, and that the blessed time might come when His chosen people should again be grafted into their own Olive Tree, and all Israel might be saved.

March 6. It rained much. Water us, O Lord, we beseech Thee, with the dew of Thy heavenly benediction.

March 13. Blessed be God, this is the most comfortable day I have had since I came last aboard; slept better than usual; was enabled to compose freely; perceived my appetite to return; was enlarged much in intercession, and found I had reason to give thanks for my late indisposition. Oh how gently does my gracious Master deal with me. Though sorrow may endure for a night, yet joy cometh in the morning. Lord, grant that I may spend that health Thou hast now restored to me to Thy honour and service! It is good for me that I have been a little chastised;

for who knows but I might otherwise have perished by being lifted up above measure with my last success? Lord give me humility, though it be through sufferings! So shall Thy blessings never prove my ruin.

March 16. Was much strengthened in my present undertaking, by reading the story of Ezra, and joined and intercession with those who set apart this day as a day of fasting and prayer for the sins of the nation to which we belong.

March 17. Last night God sent us a fair wind, and we began to sail pleasantly. I was comforted on every side, and enabled to intercede fervently for all mankind. Oh, that the love of God and man was shed abroad in my heart!

March 21. Though God gives me so much comfort, yet my dear England friends are seldom out of my mind; though absent in body I am present with them in spirit. The Lord direct my way unto them, and grant if ever I return it may be in the fullness of the blessing of the Gospel of peace.

March 30.

Renew Thy likeness, Lord, in me,
Lowly and gentle may I be,
No charms but these to Thee are dear;
No anger mayst Thou ever find,
No pride in my unruffled mind,
But faith and heaven-born peace be there.

April 8. We all, I trust, are resolved to put my afternoon's text into practice, and are determined not to know anything save Jesus Christ, and Him crucified. Grant this, O Father, for Thy dear Son's sake. Oh that I knew how to be thankful! Oh that Heaven and earth would join with me in praising God! For

I would not, Lord, alone,
Thy praises celebrate,

I'd call the blessed angels down
I'd move the world's united state,
Till they in fervent songs,
Thy gracious acts relate.

April 18. Spent most of these days in writing to my dear friends in England, and in particular supplication for direction how to act in the land whither I am going. The thoughts of my own weakness, and the greatness of those trials which I must necessarily meet with, fill me with holy fear. But wherefore do I fear? The Eternal Almighty I AM hath and will no doubt protect me.

October 22. At the desire of the Captain, preached my sermon on rash anger, having hitherto been used to expound only. In the Lesson were these remarkable words, "Return to thy own house, and show how great things God has done unto thee." And again, "It came to pass that when Jesus was returned, the people gladly received Him, for they were all waiting for Him." These last words were remarkably pressed upon me at Savannah, when I was consulting God by prayer, whether it was His will that I should go to England. Thus God's Word is in particular cases as well as in general, a light unto our feet, and a lantern unto our paths.

November 1. This afternoon, about 4 o'clock, as I was in secret, humbling myself before God, interceding for my friends, and had been praying for a fair wind, and assistance in the great work lying before me, news was brought that the wind was fair; which put me in mind of the angel's being sent to Daniel, to tell him his prayer was heard, when he was humbling his soul with fasting, and praying for the peace and restoration of Jerusalem. Indeed I cannot say, I have purposely, for these three weeks, eaten no pleasant food, or fasted as he did; but our food is so salty that I dare eat but little, so that I am now literally fasting often. Oh, that I may improve this blessed season for humiliation and extraordinary acts of devotion, that I may be duly prepared to approve myself a faithful minister of Jesus Christ, whether by honour or dishonour, by evil report or good report.

November 11. My outward man sensibly decayeth, but the spiritual man, I trust, is renewed day by day. I have besought the Lord many times to send us a fair wind; but now I see He does not think fit to answer me. I am wholly resigned, knowing that His grace will be sufficient for me, and that His time is best. Our ship is much out of repair, and our food by no means enough to support nature in an ordinary way, being of the most indifferent kind, too — an ounce or two of salt-beef, a pint of muddy water, and a cake made of flour and skimmings of the pot. I think often on Him who preserved Moses in the ark of the bulrushes. So long as I look upwards my faith will not fail.

It pities me often to see my brethren lying in the dust, as they have done these many weeks, and exposed to such straits; for God knows both their souls and bodies are dear unto me. But thanks be to God, they bear up well, and I hope we shall all now learn to endure hardships, like good soldiers of Jesus Christ.

November 14. At my first coming into our inn [in Ireland], we kneeled down and prayed, and again at night sang psalms, and prayed with the Captain and several of my shipmates — the first time, I believe, the room was ever put to such a use by a ship's crew and their captain.

November 21. As far as I can find by all I converse with, they place religion [in Ireland] in being of the Protestant or Roman Catholic communion, and are quite ignorant of the nature of inward purity and holiness of heart. Lord, the Christian world is cast into a deep sleep; send forth, I beseech Thee, some faithful and true pastors to awaken them out of it.

December 8.

Give me Thy strength, O God of power,
Then let winds blow, or thunders roar,
Thy faithful witness will I be —
'Tis fix'd! I can do all through Thee!

How God Answers Prayer

Unknown Christian

For man fully to understand God and all His dealings with us is an utter impossibility. "O the depth of the riches both of the wisdom and the knowledge of God! How unsearchable are his judgments, and his ways past tracing out!" (Rom. 11:33.) True, but we need not make difficulties where none exist. If God has all power and all knowledge, surely prayer has no difficulties, though occasionally there may be perplexities. We cannot discover God's method, but we know something of His manner of answering prayer.

But at the very outset may we remind ourselves how little we know about ordinary things? Mr. Edison, whose knowledge is pretty profound, wrote in August, 1921, "We don't know the millionth part of one percent about anything. We don't know what water is. We don't know what light is. We don't know what gravitation is. We don't know what enables us to keep on our feet to stand up. We don't know what electricity is. We don't know what heat is. We don't know anything about magnetism. We have a lot of hypotheses, but that is all." But we do not allow our ignorance about all these things to deprive us of their use! We do not know much about prayer, but surely this need not prevent us from praying! We do know what our Lord has taught us about prayer. And we do know that He has sent the Holy Spirit to teach us all things (John 14:26). How, then, does God answer prayer?

One way is just this: He reveals His mind to those who pray. His

149

Holy Spirit puts fresh ideas into the minds of praying people. We are quite aware that the devil and his angels are busy enough putting bad thoughts into our minds. Surely, then, God and His holy angels can give us good thoughts? Even poor, weak, sinful men and women can put good thoughts into the minds of others. That is what we try to do in writing! We do not stop to think what a wonderful thing it is that a few peculiar-shaped black marks on this white paper can uplift and inspire, or depress and cast down, or even convict of sin! But, to an untutored savage, it is a stupendous miracle. Moreover, you and I can often read people's thoughts or wishes from an expression on the face or a glance of the eye. Even thought transference between man and man is a commonplace today. And God can in many ways convey His thoughts to us. A remarkable instance of this was related by a speaker last year at Northfield Bible Conference. Three or four years ago, he met an old whaling captain who told him this story.

> A good many years ago, I was sailing in the desolate seas off Cape Horn, hunting whales. One day we were beating directly south in the face of a hard wind. We had been tacking this way and that all the morning, and were making very little headway. About 11 o'clock, as I stood at the wheel, the idea suddenly came into my mind, "Why batter the ship against these waves? There are probably as many whales to the north as to the south. Suppose we run with the wind instead of against it?" In response to that sudden idea I changed the course of the ship, and began to sail north instead of south. One hour later, at noon, the lookout at the masthead shouted, "Boats ahead!" Presently we overtook four lifeboats, in which were fourteen sailors, the only survivors of the crew of a ship which had burned to the water's edge ten days before. Those men had been adrift in their boats ever since, praying God frantically for rescue; and we arrived just in time to save them. They could not have survived another day.

Then the old whaler added, "I don't know whether you believe in religion or not, but I happen to be a Christian. I have begun every day of my life with prayer that God would use me to help someone else, and I am convinced that God, that day, put the idea into my mind to change the course of my ship. That idea was the means of saving fourteen lives."

God has many things to say to us. He has many thoughts to put into our minds. We are apt to be so busy doing His work that we do not stop to listen to His Word. Prayer gives God the opportunity of speaking to us and revealing His will to us. May our attitude often be: "Speak, Lord; Thy servant heareth."

God answers other prayers by putting new thoughts into the minds of those we pray for. At a series of services dealing with the Victorious Life, the writer one afternoon urged the congregation to "makeup" their quarrels if they really desired a holy life. One lady went straight home, and after very earnest prayer wrote to her sister, with whom, owing to some disagreement, she had had nothing to do for twenty years! Her sister was living thirty miles away. The very next morning the writer of that note received a letter from that very sister asking forgiveness and seeking reconciliation. The two letters had crossed in the post. While the one sister was praying to God for the other, God was speaking to that other sister, putting into her mind the desire for reconciliation.

You may say, Why did not God put that desire there before? It may be that He foresaw that it would be useless for the distant sister to write asking forgiveness until the other sister was also willing to forgive. The fact remains that, when we pray for others, somehow or other it opens the way for God to influence those we pray for. God needs our prayers, or He would not beg us to pray.

A little time back, at the end of a weekly prayer meeting, a godly woman begged those present to pray for her husband, who would never go near a place of worship. The leader suggested that they should continue in prayer then and there. Most earnest prayers were offered up. Now, the husband was devoted to his wife, and frequently came to meet her. He did so that night, and arrived at the hall while the prayer meeting was still in progress. God put it into his mind to open the door and wait inside—a thing he had never done before. As he sat on a chair near the door, leaning his head upon his hand, he overheard those earnest petitions. During the homeward walk he said, "Wife, who was the man they were praying for tonight?" "Oh," she replied, "it is the husband of one of our workers." "Well, I am quite sure he will be saved," said he; "God must answer prayers like that." A little later in the evening he again asked, "Who was the man they were praying for?" She replied in similar terms as before. On retiring to rest he could not sleep. He was under deep conviction of sin. Awaking his wife, he begged her to pray for him.

How clearly this shows us that when we pray, God can work! God could have prompted that man to enter that prayer meeting any week. But had he done so it is a question whether any good at all would have come from it. When once those earnest, heartfelt petitions were being offered up on his behalf God saw that they would have a mighty influence upon that poor man.

It is when we pray that God can help us in our work and strengthen our resolves. For we can answer many of our own prayers. One bitter winter a prosperous farmer was praying that God would keep a neighbor from starving. When the family prayers were over, his little boy said, "Father, I don't think I should have troubled God about that." "Why not?" he asked. "Because it would be easy enough for you to see that they don't starve!" There is not the slightest doubt that if we pray for others we shall also try to help them.

A young convert asked his vicar to give him some Christian work. "Have you a chum?" "Yes," replied the boy. "Is he a Christian?" "No, he is as careless as I was." "Then go and ask him to accept Christ as his Savior." "Oh, no!" said the lad, "I could never do that. Give me anything but that." "Well," said the vicar, "promise me two things: that you will not speak to him about his soul, and that you will pray to God twice daily for his conversion." "Why, yes, I'll gladly do that," answered the boy. Before a fortnight was up he rushed round to the vicarage. "Will you let me off my promise? I must speak to my chum!" he cried. When he began to pray God could give him strength to witness. Communion with God is essential before we can have real communion with our fellow-man. My belief is that men so seldom speak to others about their spiritual condition because they pray so little for them.

The writer has never forgotten how his faith in prayer was confirmed when, as a lad of thirteen, he earnestly asked God to enable him on a certain day to secure twenty new subscribers for missions overseas. Exactly twenty new names were secured before night closed in.

The consciousness that God would grant that prayer was an incentive to eager effort, and gave an unwonted courage in approaching others.

A cleric in England suggested to his people that they should each day pray for the worst man or woman and then go to them and tell them about Jesus. Only six agreed to do so. On arrival home he began to pray. Then he said, "I must not leave this to my people. I must take it up myself. I don't know the bad people. I'll have to go out and enquire." Approaching a rough-looking man at a street corner, he asked, "Are you the worst man in this district?" "No, I'm not." "Would you mind telling me who is?" "I don't mind. You'll find him at No. 7, down that street."

He knocked at No. 7 and entered. "I'm looking for the worst man in my parish. They tell me it might be you?" "Whoever told you that? Fetch him here, and I'll show him who's the worst man! No, there are lots worse than me." "Well, who is the worst man you know?" "Everybody knows him. He lives at the end house in that court. He's the worst man." So down the court he went and knocked at the door. A surly voice cried, "Come in!"

There were a man and his wife. "I hope you'll excuse me, but I'm the minister of the chapel along the round. I'm looking for the worst man in my district, because I have something to tell him. Are you the worst man?" The man turned to his wife and said, "Lass, tell him what I said to you five minutes ago." "No, tell him yourself." "What were you saying?" enquired the visitor. "Well, I've been drinking for twelve weeks. I've had the D.T's and have pawned all in the house worth pawning. And I said to my wife a few minutes ago, 'Lass, this thing has to stop, and if it doesn't, I'll stop it myself; I'll go and drown myself.' Then you knocked at the door! Yes, sir, I'm the very worst man. What have you got to say to me?" "I'm here to tell you that Jesus Christ is the greatest Savior, and that He can make out of the worst man one of the best. He did it for me, and He will do it for you." "D'you think He can do it even for me?" "I'm sure He can. Kneel down and ask Him."

Not only was the poor drunkard saved from his sins, but he is to-day a radiant Christian man, bringing other drunken people to the Lord Jesus Christ.

Surely none of us finds it difficult to believe that God can, in answer to prayer, heal the body, send rain or fair weather, dispel fogs, or avert calamities.

We have to do with a God whose knowledge is infinite. He can put it into the mind of a doctor to prescribe a certain medicine, or diet, or method of cure. All the doctor's skill is from God. "He knoweth our frame" for He made it. He knows it far better than the cleverest doctor or surgeon. He made, and He can restore. We believe that God desires us to use medical skill, but we also believe that God, by His wonderful knowledge, can heal, and sometimes does heal, without human co-operation. And God must be allowed to work in His own way. We are so apt to tie God down to the way we approve of. God's aim is to glorify His name in answering our prayers. Sometimes He sees that our desire is right, but our petition wrong. St. Paul thought he could bring more glory to God if only the thorn in the flesh could be removed. God knew that he would be a better man and do better work with the thorn than without it. So God said No, No, No, to his prayer, and then explained why!

So it was with Monica, who prayed so many years for the conversion of Augustine (354-430), her licentious son. When he was determined to leave home and cross the seas to Rome she prayed earnestly, even passionately, that God would keep him by her side, and under her influence. She went down to a little chapel on the seashore to spend the night in prayer close by where the ship lay at anchor. But, when morning came, she found that the ship had sailed even while she prayed! Her petition was refused, but her real desire was granted. For it was in Rome that Augustine met the sainted Ambrose, who led him to Christ. How comforting it is to know that God knows what is best!

But we should never think it unreasonable that God should make some things dependent upon our prayers. Some people say that if God really loves us He would give us what is best for us whether we ask Him or not. Dr. Harry Fosdick (1878-1969) has so beautifully pointed out that God has left man many things to do for himself. He promises seedtime and harvest. Yet man must prepare the soil, sow, and till, and reap in order to allow God to do His share. God provides us with food and drink. But He leaves us to take, and eat, and drink. There are some things God cannot, or at least will not, do without our help. God cannot do some things unless we think. He never emblazons His truth upon the sky. The laws of science have always been there. But we must think, and experiment, and think again if we would use those laws for our own good and God's glory.

God cannot do some things unless we work. He stores the hills with marble, but He has never built a cathedral. He fills the mountains with iron ore, but He never makes a needle or a locomotive. He leaves that to us. We must work.

If, then, God has left many things dependent upon man's thinking and working, why should He not leave some things dependent upon man's praying? He has done so. "Ask and ye shall receive." And there are some things God will not give us unless we ask. Prayer is one of the three ways in which man can cooperate with God; and the greatest of these is prayer.

Men of power are without exception men of prayer. God bestows His Holy Spirit in His fullness only on men of prayer. And it is through the operation of the Spirit that answers to prayer come. Every believer has the Spirit of Christ dwelling in him. For "if any have not the Spirit of Christ, he is none of his." But a man of prevailing prayer must be filled with the Spirit of God.

A lady missionary wrote recently that it used to be said of Praying Hyde (1865-1912) that he never spoke to an unconverted man but that he was soundly converted. But if he ever did fail at first to touch a heart for God, he went back to his room and wrestled in prayer till he was shown what it was in himself that had hindered his being used by God. Yes, when we are filled with the Spirit of God, we cannot help influencing others God-ward. But, to have power with men, we must have power with God.

The momentous question for you and me is not, however, "How does God answer prayer?" The question is, "Do I really pray?" What a marvelous power God places at our disposal! Do we for a moment think that anything displeasing to God is worth our while holding on to? Fellow Christian, trust Christ wholly, and you will find Him wholly true.

Let us give God the chance of putting His mind into us, and we shall never doubt the power of prayer again.[1]

26

Spirit Divine, Attend our Prayer

Andrew Reed

Spirit divine, attend our prayer,
And make our heart Thy home;
Descend with all Thy gracious power;
Come, Holy Spirit, come.

Come as the light! to us reveal
The truth we long to know;
Reveal the narrow path of right,
The way of duty show.

Come as the fire and purge our hearts
Like sacrificial flame,
Till our whole souls an offering be
In love's redeeming name.

Come as the dew, and sweetly bless
This consecrated hour;
May barrenness rejoice to own
Thy fertilizing power.

Come as the dove, and spread Thy wings,

The wings of peaceful love;
And let Thy Church on earth become
Blest as Thy Church above.

Come as the wind, O Breath of God!
O Pentecostal grace!
Come, make Thy great salvation known,
Wide as the human race.

Spirit divine, attend our prayer;
Make a lost world Thy home;
Descend with all thy gracious powers,
O come, great Spirit, come.[1]

Biographical Sketches

Anselm of Canterbury (1033-1109) was born in Acosta, Italy. In 1059 he entered the famous monastery of Bec, of which he became abbot in 1078. He became Archbishop of Canterbury in 1093. Most famously, in the *Proslogion* (*Addition*), Anselm proposed the famous Ontological Argument, according to which God is understood as "that than which nothing greater can be conceived." The Being so conceived must necessarily exist in reality as well as in thought, he argued, since otherwise it would in fact be possible to conceive something greater—namely, something exactly similar except that it really does exist. Thus, at least for Anselmian believers guided by a prior faith, God must truly exist as the simple, unified source of all perfections, a reality that excludes corruption, imperfection, and deception of every sort.

J. Sidlow Baxter (1903-1999) was born in Australia and grew up in Lancashire, England. He attended Spurgeon's Theological College in London and was a pastor in Scotland and England. He is the author of over thirty books. "When I was five I went with my mother to an evangelistic meeting. After preaching, the missioner gave the 'invitation' and I was one of several who went out across a corridor to anterooms where counselors waited to help us. The lady who dealt with me was a near neighbor. With wonderful diplomacy she said, "Oh Sid, how delighted we are to see you coming to receive Jesus!" To a five-year-old that meant much. . . . Afterward I went back to the main hall, to an addendum meeting in which testimonies were being given. When a pause came I stood, and my little voice piped out, 'Tonight I have taken Jesus as my Savior, and such a burden has rolled away . . .' I got no further.

Sitting in front of my mother and me were two maiden ladies, one of whom loudly whispered, 'How ridiculous! A mere child talking like that!' My mind was confused. My cheeks crimsoned. I faltered and sank down humiliated. This conversion business suddenly seemed an adult sham. From then onward I just could not believe. I shut Jesus out of my life, and grew up a thorough worldling." Baxter later fully came to Christ at the age of sixteen and preached the gospel for seventy years, traveling around the world.

Horatius Bonar (1808-1889) had a passionate heart for revival and was a friend and supporter of several revivalists. He was brother to the more well-known Andrew Bonar. His gifts for expressing theological truths in fluent verse form are evident in all his best-known hymns, but in addition he was also blessed with a deep understanding of doctrinal principles. After almost twenty years laboring in the Scottish borders at Kelso, Bonar moved back to Edinburgh in 1866 to be minister at the Chalmers Memorial Chapel (now renamed St. Catherine's Argyle Church). He continued his ministry for a further twenty years helping to arrange D. L. Moody's meetings in Edinburgh in 1873 and being appointed moderator of the Free Church of Scotland ten years later.

Samuel Chadwick (1860-1932) was one of English Methodism's finest preachers. Born in Burnley in a strong Methodist home, as a lad he worked in a cotton mill twelve hours a day. He was converted at the age of ten, and immediately began praying three times a day. He began preaching at the age of sixteen. He became a lay pastor at Stacksteads when he was twenty-one. At the time he had fifteen sermons; unfortunately no conversions resulted from his sermons and so he burned them. He entered into what he referred to as a "crisis of obedience." Thereafter, he saw multitudes of conversions. He served several local churches, and in time, became known for his outdoor preaching. He served as the editor of the *Joyful News Magazine* for twenty-five years. At the age of forty-seven, he became an instructor in biblical and theological studies at Cliff College, Leeds. Later he became the principal of the college. Two of his most known books are *The Path of Prayer* and *Pentecost*.

William Cowper (1731-1800) was born in Great Berkhamsted, England; however his older siblings died and his mother died when William was not yet six years old. Many biographers attribute Cowper's mental instability to the death of his mother in childbirth in 1737. This is only speculation inasmuch as Cowper never speaks to the cause of his times of despair and severe melancholy. However, in this hymn, "God Moves in A Mysterious Way," he certainly addresses the often mysterious and dark providences of God. Cowper's family is noteworthy for its literary and ecclesiastical standing. His father had served as chaplain to King George II; but also notable is that his mother was a descendent of John Donne who served as Dean of St. Paul's Cathedral and was a recognized poet. In the early 1760s he was admitted to what was termed then a "lunatic asylum." Yet even in this asylum, the sovereign God came to him, and while he was a patient he came to faith in Christ and was converted. This faith would be the anchor of his soul throughout his life. In 1867, a relationship would begin that would be of benefit for not only Cowper's soul, but for the Christian church throughout the ages. It was at this time that John Newton, the noted pastor, theologian, and hymn writer, invited Cowper to come and live in Olney, a small community in Buchinghamshire, England.

Frederick William Faber (1814-1863) was a son of an Anglican clergyman and a graduate of Oxford, was ordained an Anglican minister, and became Rector of Elton in 1843. Three years later, he identified with Roman Catholicism. Faber published a number of prose works, and three volumes of hymns. He was founder of the Wilfridians, a religious society living in common without vows. Faber was elected fellow of University College, Oxford, in 1837. He is remembered chiefly as a hymnist, some of his most popular hymns in Protestantism are "Faith of our Fathers," "I Worship, Thee, Sweet Will of God," "My God, How Wonderful Thou Art," and "Workman of God."

François Fénelon (1651-1715) was a French Catholic priest. Anxious about his spiritual life, Fénelon sought an answer from the Quietist school of prayer. Introduced in October 1688 to Quietism's leading exponent, Mme Guyon, Fénelon sought from her some means of personally experiencing the God whose existence he had intellectually assented to, but his search for spiritual peace was short-lived. Bishop Jacques Bénigne Bossuet and other influential people at court attacked Mme Guyon's teaching, and a document investigating Quietism's doubtful orthodoxy even obtained Fénelon's signature. When Bossuet, however, next launched a personal attack on Mme Guyon, Fénelon responded with "Explanation of the Sayings of the Saints on the Interior Life." Defending Mme Guyon's integrity, Fénelon not only lost Bossuet's friendship but also exposed himself to Bossuet's public denunciation. As a result, Fénelon's *Maximes des saints* was condemned by the pope, and he was exiled to his diocese.

Ole Hallesby (1879-1961) was one of Norway's leading Christian teachers and devotional writers. During World War II he was imprisoned for his resistance to the Nazi regime. He worked as a seminary professor in Oslo until his death. While having a background in the liberal theology, he experienced a radical conversion, which also made him a determined enemy of the liberal phalanx. He was indeed both fearless and outspoken, and led an intelligent campaign against the liberals, which won him confidence both from conservative ministers and from the lay organizations.

Andrew Murray (1828-1917) was born in Cape Town, South Africa, who became a noted missionary leader, author, and revivalist. His father was a Scottish Presbyterian serving the Dutch Reformed Church of South Africa, and his mother had connections with both French Huguenots and German Lutherans. This background to some extent explains his ecumenical spirit. He was educated at Aberdeen University, Scotland, and at Utrecht University in the Netherlands. After ordination in 1848 he served pastorates. He helped to found what are now the University College of the Orange Free State and the Stellenbosch Seminary. He served as Moderator of the Cape Synod of the Dutch Reformed Church and was president of both the YMCA (1865) and the South Africa General Mission (1888-1917), now the Africa Evangelical Fellowship. He was one of the chief promoters of the call to missions in South Africa. Murray is best known today for his devotional writings, which place great emphasis on the need for a rich, personal devotional life. Several of his books have become devotional classics. Among these are *Abide*

in Christ, Absolute Surrender, With Christ in the School of Prayer, The
Spirit of Christ and Waiting on God.

Stephen F. Olford (1918-2004) was born in Zambia as the son of missionaries. He spent his college years in the United Kingdom and a crisis experience led to his full surrender to the Lord and his call into the ministry. After receiving ministry training, Olford was appointed an Army Scripture Reader during World War II, and he launched a Young Peoples Christian fellowship in Newport, South Wales. After the war, Stephen was involved in extensive evangelistic and preaching ministry throughout the U. K. and overseas. In 1953, Dr. Olford's years of pastoral ministry began by serving the Duke Street Baptist Church in Richmond, Surrey England (1953-1959) and then the Calvary Baptist Church in New York City (1959-1973). Cliff Barrows, long-time associate of Billy Graham, wrote upon learning of Dr. Olford's death: "Stephen Olford left his footprint upon my heart and life, as he has on people around the world; My late wife and I heard Stephen preach on the Spirit-filled life. It really challenged us and changed our lives as we looked forward to six months of ministry in England."

Andrew Reed (1787-1862) was born in London and educated for the Congregational Ministry at Hackney College, London. He was first the pastor of the New Road Chapel, St. George's-in-the-East, and then of the Wycliffe Chapel, which was built through his leadership in 1830. He was actively involved in many humanitarian concerns: the founder of "The London Orphan Asylum," "The Asylum for Fatherless Children," "The Asylum for Idiots" "The Infant Orphan Asylum," and "The Hospital for Incurables." Dr. Reed is more fully known today by the hymns he authors, numbering twenty-one. One of his most popular hymns is "Holy Ghost, With Light Divine."

Gilbert Shaw. We know very little about Shaw. What we do know is that he was a minister and a contemporary of Sir Henry S. Lunn (1859-1939). Lunn thought so highly of Shaw's little booklet, *A Pilgrim's Chapbook: The Pattern of the Master*, that he included it in his book, *The Secret of the Saints*. In acknowledging his gratitude to Shaw for granting him permission to reprint his booklet of prayers and meditations, he wrote: "I am greatly indebted to the generosity of the Reverend Gilbert Shaw for allowing me to publish this."

Oswald J. Smith (1889-1986) was a Canadian pastor, author, and missions advocate. He founded The People's Church in Toronto in 1928. Smith attended the Toronto Bible Training School, the Manitoba Presbyterian College in Winnipeg, and the McCormick Seminary in Chicago. He was ordained as a minister of the Presbyterian Church of Canada in 1918; however, he resigned from the Presbyterian Church, believing he was to found a non-denominational church, which merged with a small Christian and Missionary Alliance congregation in 1921. In 1928, he started another independent church in Toronto, the People's Church. Over the course of eighty years, in addition to preaching thousands of sermons, he wrote thirty-five books (with translations into 128 languages), as well as twelve thousand poems, of which one hundred have been set to music, including "Deeper and Deeper" and "Then Jesus Came."

Charles Haddon Spurgeon (1834-1892) was England's best known preacher for most of the second half of the nineteenth century. In 1854, just four years after his conversion, Spurgeon, then only twenty, became pastor of London's famed New Park Street Church. The congregation quickly outgrew their building, moved to Exeter Hall, then to Surrey Music Hall. In these venues Spurgeon frequently preached to audiences numbering more than ten thousand — all in the days before electronic amplification. In 1861 the congregation moved permanently to the newly constructed Metropolitan Tabernacle. Spurgeon's printed works are voluminous.

Ralph I. Tilley was converted at the age of sixteen. He has served Christ and his church as a pastor for thirty-eight years, as the editor of *Life in the Spirit* journal for twenty years, and as a professor of New Testament Studies at the Bible college, seminary, and university levels. He holds a Bachelor of Theology degree from God's Bible School & College, Master of Arts in Religion degree from Andrews University, and a Doctor of Religious Studies degree from Trinity Theological Seminary. Ralph is currently the online editor of *Life in the Spirit Journal*, and is engaged in a writing ministry. He and his wife Emily reside in Sellersburg, Indiana.

R. A. Torrey (1856-1928) was an American evangelist, pastor, educator, and writer. He graduated from Yale University in 1875 and Yale Divinity School in 1878. Following graduation, Torrey became a Congregational minister in Garrettsville, Ohio, in 1878, marrying Clara Smith there in October 1879. After further studies of theology at Leipzig University and Erlangen University in 1882-1883, Torrey joined Dwight L. Moody in his evangelistic work in Chicago in 1889, and became superintendent of the Bible Institute of the Chicago Evangelization Society (now Moody Bible Institute); he served as the first academic dean of what is now known as Biola University. His pastorates included Chicago Avenue Church (now Moody Memorial Church) and Church of the Open Door, Los Angeles. He died at home in Asheville, North Carolina, on October 26, 1928, having preached the world over and having left a legacy of thousands of converts to Christ and over forty books.

A. W. Tozer (1897-1963). While on his way home from an Akron, Ohio tire company where he worked as a teen, Tozer overheard a street preacher say, "If you don't know how to be saved . . . just call on God." Upon returning home, Tozer climbed into the attic and heeded the preacher's advice. In 1919, five years after his decision to follow Christ, and without formal theological training, Tozer accepted an offer to pastor his first church. This began forty-four fruitful years of ministry, thirty of which he served as pastor of the Southside Alliance Church in Chicago (1928 to 1959). His final years were spent pastoring the Avenue Road (Alliance) Church in Toronto, Canada. Prayer was of vital personal importance for Tozer. "His preaching as well as his writings were but extensions of his prayer life," comments his biographer, James L. Snyder in the book, *In Pursuit of God: The Life of A. W. Tozer.* "He had the ability to make his listeners face themselves in the light of what God was saying to them."

George Verwer, while still in college, established the ministry that became Operation Mobilization. George had come to faith in high school as a result of a praying woman in his neighborhood in New Jersey. She prayed for the students at the nearby high school, asking God to save them and send some of them out as missionaries. She prayed that George would come to faith in Christ, and she mailed him a Gospel of John. After reading the Gospel for three years, George went to hear Billy Graham speak at a Jack Wyrtzen event in 1955. He committed himself to Christ and very soon led many people in his school to faith. In college, first at Maryville College in Maryville, Tennessee, and then at Moody Bible Institute in Chicago, George challenged other students to pray radically for countries of the world and to go as missionaries. In 1957, he and two friends used their summer break to take a truckload of Gospels to Mexico on their first mission trip. That trip was the birth of what would become Operation Mobilization.

George Whitefield (1714-1770) was the eighteenth century's "Billy Graham" in both America and Great Britain. In 1732 at age seventeen, he entered Pembroke College at Oxford. He was gradually drawn into a group called the "Holy Club" where he met John and Charles Wesley. Charles Wesley loaned him the book, *The Life of God in the Soul of Man*. The reading of this book, after a long and painful struggle which even affected him physically, finally resulted in Whitefield's conversion in 1735. He said many years later: "I know the place. . . . Whenever I go to Oxford, I cannot help running to the spot where Jesus Christ first revealed himself to me and gave me the new birth." Whitefield was an anointed preacher from the beginning. Within a year it was said that "his voice startled England like a trumpet blast." For thirty-four years his preaching resounded throughout England and America. In his preaching ministry he crossed the Atlantic thirteen times and became known as the "apostle of the British empire." Though estranged from John Wesley for a time because of their doctrinal differences, he requested that Wesley preach his funeral, which he did.

Biographical Sources: Anselm, ccel.org/ccel/anselm. **Baxter:** christian bookpreviews.com. **Bonar:** ccel.org/mt/mobile/browseauthorInfo? id=bonar. **Chadwick:** path2prayer.com/.../samuel-chadwick-great-man -of-the-holy-spirit. **Cowper:** leben.us/volume-6...6.../327-william-cowper-the-evangelical-poet. **Faber:** itannica.com/EBchecked/topic/ 199664/Frederick-William-Faber. **Fénelon:** Britannica.com/.../topic/.../

Francois-de-Salignac-de-La-Mothe-Fenelon. **Hallesby**: books.google. com/books?isbn=080662700X. **Murray**: ccel.org/ccel/murray. **Olford**: http://www.oneplace.com/ministries/encounter-olford-ministries/ read/. **Reed**: hymnary.org/text spirit_divine_ attend_our_prayers. **Shaw**: The Secret of the Saints , published by Macmillan, New York, 1933. Smith: hymnary.org/person/. **Spurgeon**: Spurgeon.org/aboutsp. htm. Torrey: ccel.org/ccel/torrey. **Tozer**: cmalliance.org. **Verwer**: omu-sa.org/about-us/george-verwer. **Whitefield**: books.google.com/books? isbn=0882704737.

Acknowledgements

A Prayer for God's Purity, quoted by Henry S. Lunn. This prayer-poem is taken from *The Secret of the Saints*, published by Macmillan, New York, 1933. In the public domain.

A Prayer to Christ by Anselm of Canterbury. Anselm. This prayer-poem is taken from *The Prayers and Meditations of Saint Anselm with the Proslogion*, with an Introduction by Benedicta Ward, S.L.G. Published by Penguin Classics 1973; © 1973 Benedicta Ward. Adapted for publication. In the public domain.

Distractions in Prayer by Frederick William Faber. This prayer-poem is in the public domain.

How to Pray by R. A. Torrey. This chapter is taken from *The Treasury of R. A. Torrey*, with Introduction by George T. B. Davis. Published by Baker Book House, Grand Rapids, Michigan; reprinted 1967. In the public domain.

On Maintaining a Life of Prayer by François Fénelon. This chapter is taken from *Talking With God: François Fénelon*, Contemporary English Edition, edited by Hal M. Helms and Robert J. Edmonson, Copyright © 2009 by The Community of Jesus. Used by permission of Paraclete Press.

Praying in the Spirit by Samuel Chadwick. This chapter is taken from Samuel Chadwick, *The Path of Prayer*, published by Hodder and Stroughton, London. Used by permission of Cliff College, England.

Spirit Divine by Andrew Reed. This prayer-poem is in the public domain.

Submission by William Cowper. This prayer-poem is in the public domain.

The Man God Uses by Oswald J, Smith. This chapter is taken from Oswald J. Smith, *The Man God Uses, published by* Marshall, Morgan & Scott, London, 1942). In the public domain.

The Meaning of Prayer by O. Hallesby. This chapter is taken from *Prayer*, O. Hallesby, trans. by Clarence J. Carlsen; Augsburg Fortress Publishing House, Minneapolis, MN. Used by permission.

The Spirit of Supplication by Andrew Murray. This chapter is taken from Andrew Murray, *The Ministry of Intercession*, published by Bethany House Publishers, Minneapolis, reprinted 1981. In the public domain.

The Prayer Life of George Whitefield. This chapter is taken from *George Whitefield's Journals, published by* The Banner of Truth Trust, Carlisle, PA. In the public domain.

The Prayers of the Saints by Charles H. Spurgeon. This chapter is taken from a sermon preached on May 19, 1872. *The Metropolitan Tabernacle Pulpit,* 18:105. In the public domain.

The Praying Plumber by A. W. Tozer. This chapter is taken from A. W. Tozer, *The Praying Plumber of Lisburn.* Published by Christian Publications; Harrisburg, PA. In the public domain.

We Thank Thee, Lord, for Using Us by Horatius Bonar. This prayer-poem is in the public domain.

Whatever Happened to the Prayer Meeting by George Verwer. This chapter is taken from georgeverwer.com. In the public domain.

Will and Emotions by J. Sidlow Baxter. This chapter has appeared in various venues and is in the public domain.

Endnotes

Introduction

1. Howard Taylor, *Hudson Taylor and the China Inland Mission* (London: The Religious Tract Society, 1921), 625. Retrieved from ttps://ia60031. us.archive.org/1/items/hudsontaylorchin00tayl/hudsontaylorlorchin 00tayl.pdf.
2. Andrew Murray, *With Christ in the School of Prayer* (Old Tappan, NJ: 1953), 144.
3. Taken from "Prayer is the Soul's Sincere Desire" by James Montgomery.

Chapter 1: This Thing Called Prayer

1. James M. Boice, *Foundations of the Christian Faith,* rev. ed. (Downers Grove, IL: InterVarsity Press, 1986), 483.
2. Dallas Willard, *The Spirit of the Disciplines* (San Francisco: Harper Collins Publishers, 1988), 184.
3. W. Bingham Hunter, *The God Who Hears* (Downers Grove, IL: InterVarsity Press, 1986), 13.
4. James Hastings, *The Great Christian Doctrines, The Doctrine of Prayer* (Edinburgh: T. & T. Clark, 1915), 21.
5. James L. Garrett, Jr., *Systematic Theology*, vol. 2, 2nd ed. (North Richland Hills, TX: Bibal Press, 2001), 429-447.
6. Unless otherwise indicated, all Scripture quotations in this chapter are taken from *The Holy Bible, English Standard Version* (ESV).
7. Garrett, Jr. 431-432.
8. James Montgomery, "Prayer is the Soul's Sincere Desire."
9. Wayne Grudem, *Systematic Theology* (Grand Rapids: Zondervan, 1994), 376.
10. Ibid., 377.
11. Richard J. Foster, *Celebration of Discipline* (San Francisco: Harper Collins Publishers, 1998), 33.
12. Ibid., 35.
13. Millard J. Erickson, *Christian Theology*, 2nd ed. (Grand Rapids: Baker

Books, 1998), all quotes in this chapter are from pp. 430-431.

14. O. Hallesby, *Prayer* (Minneapolis: Augsburg Publishing House, 1931), 158.

15. Ibid., 159.

16. Karl Barth, *Prayer*, 2nd ed., Don E. Saliers, ed. (Philadelphia: The Westminster Press, 1985), 35.

17. Samuel Chadwick, *The Path of Prayer* (London: Hodder and Stroughton, 1963), 38.

18. Carl F. H. Henry, *God Who Stands and Stays, God, Revelation and Authority*, vol. VI (Wheaton, IL: Crossway Books, 1983), 482.

19. W. T. Purkiser, Richard S. Taylor, Willard H. Taylor, *God, Man & Salvation* (Kansas City: Beacon Hill Press, 1977), 519.

20. Herman Ridderbos, *The Gospel According to John*, trans. by John Vriend (Grand Rapids: Wm. B. Eerdmans Publishing Co., 1997), 498-499.

21. Grudem, 384.

22. John Newton, "Come, My Soul, Thy Suit Prepare. "

Chapter 2: *A Prayer to Christ*

1. This prayer is taken from Anselm, *St. Anselm's Book of Meditations and Prayers* (London: Burns and Oates, 1872), 148-150. Retrieved from http://www.saintsbooks.net/books/St.%20Anselm%20of%20Canterbury%20-%20Meditations%20and%20Prayers.pdf.

Chapter 3: The Meaning of Prayer

1. This chapter is taken from O. Hallesby, *Prayer*, trans. by Clarence J. Carlsen (Minneapolis: Augsburg Publishing House, 1959), 125-134.

Chapter 4: How to Pray

1. This chapter is taken from R. A. Torrey, *The Treasury of R. A. Torrey*, (Grand Rapids: Baker Book House, reprinted 1967), 100-102.

Chapter 5: The Prayers of the Saints

1. This chapter is taken from Charles H. Spurgeon, *The Metropolitan Tabernacle Pulpit* (London: Passmore & Alabaster, n. d.), 18:105.

Chapter 6: *A Prayer for God's Purity*

1. Quoted by Henry S. Lunn, *The Secret of the Saints* (New York: The Macmillan Co., 1933), 211-213.

Chapter 7: The Prayer Life of Jesus

1. Unless otherwise indicated, all Scripture quotations in this chapter are taken from *The Holy Bible, English Standard Version*.

2. Howard Taylor, *Hudson Taylor and the China Inland Mission* (London: The Religious Tract Society, 1921), 624. Retrieved from https://ia60031.us.archive.org/1/items/hudsontaylorchin00tayl/hudsontaylorchin00tayl.pdf.

3. Taken from "Fill Me Now" by Elwood H. Stokes.
4. Taken from "Arise, My Soul, Arise" by Charles Wesley.
5. Andrew Bonar, *Robert Murray M'Cheyne* (London: The Banner of Truth Trust, reprinted 1962 from original 1844), 179.

Chapter 8: The Praying Plumber of Lisburn
1. This chapter is taken from A. W. Tozer, *The Praying Plumber of Lisburn* (Harrisburg, PA: Christian Publications, n. d.), 4-11, 27-33.

Chapter 9: Will and Emotions
1. Dr. Baxter shared this account in many venues throughout his ministry, one of which was "Leadership Journal," April 1, 1986.

Chapter 10: *Submission*
1. This hymn originally appeared in *Olney Hymns*, first published in 1779 by John Newton. William Cowper (1731-1800), a friend of Newton's, collaborated with Newton in later editions of the Olney series.

Chapter 11: Bending Low in Prayer
1. T. S. Rendall, "The Prairie Overcomer," Sept., 1988, 2.
2. Unless otherwise indicated, all Scripture quotations in this chapter are taken from *The Holy Bible, English Standard Version.*
3. Kurt Koch, *Revival Fires in Canada*, (Grand Rapids: Kregel, 1973), 30-31.
4. Robert E. Coleman, *One Divine Moment*, (Old Tappan, NJ: Fleming H. Revell, 1970), 102.
5. James A. Stewart, *Opened Windows* (Ashville, NC: Revival Literature, reprinted 1999), 104-105.

Chapter 12: Whatever Happened to the Prayer Meeting
1. This chapter is taken from George Verwer, "Whatever Happened to the Prayer Meeting." Retrieved from http://www.georgeverwer.com/articles/prayerMeeting.pdf.

Chapter 13: The Highest Form of Christian Service
1. This chapter is taken from Oswald J. Smith, *The Man God Uses* (London: Marshall, Morgan & Scott, 1942), 108-120.

Chapter 14: *We Thank Thee, Lord, for Using Us*
1. Horatius Bonar (1808-1889) wrote over six hundred hymns. He has been called "the prince of Scottish Hymn writers."

Chapter 15: On Maintaining a Life of Prayer
1. See Matthew 7:15-20.
2. Romans 1:18 KJV.
3. Psalm 66:20 NIV.

4. This chapter is taken from François Fénelon, *Talking with God*, ed. by Hal M. Helms (Brewster, MA: Paraclete Press, 1997), 7-11.

Chapter 16: Praying in the Spirit
1. This chapter is taken from Samuel Chadwick, *The Path of Prayer* (London: Hodder and Stroughton,, n. d.), 41-45.

Chapter 17: She Prayed All Night
1. This chapter is taken from R. A. Torrey, *The Treasury of R. A. Torrey* (Grand Rapids: Baker Book House, reprinted 1967), 100-102.

Chapter 18: *Distractions in Prayer*
1. Frederick William Faber (1814-1863) was a prominent English hymn writer and theologian. In addition to publishing many books, he also composed three volumes of hymns.

Chapter 19: Drawing Near (Part 1)
1. Adam Clarke. *Clarke's Commentaries* (Nashville: Abingdon Press, n. d.), 1:57.
2. Dennis F. Kinlaw. *This Day With the Master* (Grand Rapids: Zondervan, 2002), November 16.
3. Unless otherwise indicated, all Scripture references in this chapter are taken from the *New American Standard Bible*.
4. Matthew Henry. *A Commentary on the Whole Bible*. (Old Tappan, N.J., n. d.), 1:30.
5. See Hebrews 1:4-9; 7:18-19; 8:6-13; 9:23; 4:14-5:11.
6. F. F. Bruce. *The Epistle to the Hebrews: The English Text With Introduction, Exposition and Notes*. (Grand Rapids: Wm. B. Eerdmans Publishing Co., 1964), 8.
7. "The American Heritage Dictionary of the English Language." 4th ed. (New York: Houghton Mifflin Co., 2000), 1305.
8. Taken from "Not all the Blood" by Isaac Watts.
9. Taken from "Arise, My Soul, Arise" by Charles Wesley.

Chapter 20: Drawing Near (Part 2)
1. Unless otherwise indicated, all Scripture references in this chapter are taken from the *New American Standard Bible*.
2. Taken from "When I Survey the Wondrous Cross" by Isaac Watts.
3. Taken from "Come, My Soul, Thy Suit Prepare" by John Newton.
4. Duncan Campbell, *The Price and Power of Revival* (Fort Washington, PA: Christian Literature Crusade, n. d.), 66-68.
5. William L. Lane. *Hebrews 9-13, Word Biblical Commentary*, vol. 47B. (Nashville: Thomas Nelson Publishers, 1991), 287.
6. Dennis F. Kinlaw. *Preaching in the Spirit* (Grand Rapids: Zondervan, 1985), 116-117.

7. Taken from "Arise, My Soul, Arise" by Charles Wesley.

Chapter 21: Drawing Near (Part 3)
1. Unless otherwise indicated, all Scripture references in this chapter are taken from *The Holy Bible, English Standard Version*.
2. Psalm 10:16 is only one of many references on this subject.
3. Matthew 19:28; Acts 7:49; Revelation 5:13 (one of many references in Revelation).
4. Taken from "O Worship the King" by Robert Grant.
5. See Matthew 5:17, for example.
6. See 2 Corinthians 5:10; Revelation 20:11, for example.
7. F. F. Bruce, *The Epistle to the Hebrews*. (Grand Rapids: Wm. B. Eerdmans Co., 1964), 90.
8. B. F. Westcott, *The Epistle to the Hebrews*. (Grand Rapids: Wm. B. Eerdmans Co., 1889; reprinted 1974), 106.
9. Bruce, 91.
10. See Leviticus, chapters 4 and 5.
11. Craig C. Koester, *Hebrews, The Anchor Bible*, vol. 36. (New York: Doubleday, 2001), 286.
12. Taken from "Depth of Mercy" by Charles Wesley.

Chapter 22: Drawing Near (Part 4)
1. Taken from "Saved to the Uttermost" by William J. Kirkpatrick.
2. Unless otherwise indicated, all Scripture references in this chapter are taken from *The Holy Bible, English Standard Version*.
3. Romans 4:21, 8:38; 2 Corinthians 9:8; Ephesians 3:20; Hebrews 2:18; Jude 24.
4. Thomas Cook, *New Testament Holiness* (London: Epworth Press, 1958), 127.
5. *The ESV Study Bible, English Standard Version* (Wheaton: Crossway Bibles, 208), 2372.
6. Craig C. Koester, *Hebrews, The Anchor Bible*, vol. 36. (New York: Doubleday, 2001), 365.
7. Cited by William L. Lane, *Hebrews 1-8, Word Biblical Commentary*, vol. 47A (Nashville: Thomas Nelson Publishers, 1991), 188.
8. Ralph I. Tilley.
9. F. F. Bruce, *The Epistle to the Hebrews*. (Grand Rapids: Wm. B. Eerdmans Co., 1964), 153-154.
10. Taken from "There is a Fountain Filled with Blood," by William Cowper.
11. Bruce, 154-155.
12. Quoted by F. F. Bruce, *The Epistle to the Hebrews*. (Grand Rapids: Wm. B. Eerdmans Co., 1964), 155.
13. Taken from "Arise, My Soul Arise" by Charles Wesley.

Chapter 23: The Spirit of Supplication
1. This chapter is taken from Andrew Murray, *The Ministry of Intercession*

(Minneapolis: Bethany House Publishers, originally published in 1897; edited and reprinted 1981), 74-80.

Chapter 24: The Prayer Life of George Whitefield
1.   This chapter is taken from *George Whitefield's Journals* (Carlisle, PA: The Banner of Truth Trust, originally published 1738-1741; reprinted and edited 1960).

Chapter 25: How God Answers Prayer
1.   This chapter is taken from *The Kneeling Christian,* chapter 10. It was written by an "Unknown Author," sometime before the 1930s. It has been reprinted by various individuals and publishers through the years; it is in the public domain.

Chapter 26: *Spirit Divine, Attend our Prayer*
1.   Andrew Reed (1787-1862) was an English minister and hymn writer. "He published a Supplement (1817) to Isaac Watts' hymns, which was enlarged in 1825 and called *The Hymn Book*; it included twenty-one hymn-texts by Reed and twenty anonymous texts by Reed's wife."

More books by Ralph I. Tilley

Thirsting for God (2011)

Letters from Noah (historical fiction, 2013)

The Mind of Christ by John R. MacDuff; edited reprint (2013)

A Passion for Christ (2013)

How Christ Came to Church: An Anthology of the Works of A. J. Gordon; edited reprint (2013)

Breath of God (2013)

The Christian's Vital Breath (2014)

COMING in 2014 . . .

Christ in You

Not Peace But a Sword by Vance Havner;
with Introduction by Ralph I. Tilley

The Bow in the Cloud by John R. MacDuff; edited reprint

Books available at either . . .

litsjournal.org

amazon.com

Made in the USA
Charleston, SC
01 March 2014